Anthropological Abstracts

Anthropological Abstracts

Cultural/Social Anthropology
from German-speaking countries

edited by
Ulrich Oberdiek

Volume 9. 2010

LIT

Bibliographic information published by the Deutsche Nationalbibliothek
The Deutsche Nationalbibliothek lists this publication in the Deutsche Nationalbibliografie; detailed bibliographic data are available in the Internet at http://dnb.d-nb.de.

ISBN 978-3-643-99833-0
ISSN 0173-2986

A catalogue record for this book is available from the British Library

©LIT VERLAG Dr. W. Hopf Berlin 2014
Fresnostr. 2   D-48159 Münster
Tel. +49 (0) 2 51-62 03 20   Fax +49 (0) 2 51-23 19 72
e-Mail: lit@lit-verlag.de   http://www.lit-verlag.de
In Germany: LIT Verlag Fresnostr. 2, D-48159 Münster

Tel. +49 (0) 2 51-620 32 22, Fax +49 (0) 2 51-922 60 99, E-mail: vertrieb@lit-verlag.de
In Austria: Medienlogistik Pichler-ÖBZ, e-mail: mlo@medien-logistik.at
In the UK: Global Book Marketing, e-mail: mo@centralbooks.com
In North America: International Specialized Book Services, e-mail: orders@isbs.com

Contents

Editorial

This reference journal is published once a year and announces – in English language – most of the new publications in the field of cultural/social anthropology published in the German language area (Austria, Germany, Switzerland). Since many of these publications have been written in German, and most of them are not included in major, English language abstracting services, *Anthropological Abstracts (AA)* offers an opportunity and convenient source of information for scholars who do not read German, to become aware of anthropological research and publications in these countries. Included are journal articles, monographs, anthologies, exhibition catalogs, yearbooks, etc. Occasionally, publications in English, or French, are included as well if the publisher is less well-known internationally, and if it is likely that the publication will not be noticed abroad.

Additionally, abbreviated versions of *Anthropological Abstracts* appear in the internet: www.anthropology-online.de.

Some technical remarks

This reference journal uses a flexible approach in representing publications: While in usually abstracts are supplied, for *anthologies* the Current Contents method is applied, i.e. *only* authors and titles are printed. So technically, this is a combined approach: an Abstracting Reference Journal, and the Current Contents method of listing names and titles only. However, the complete material, including those papers which appear by title only, has been thoroughly indexed.

Abstracts supplied by authors are marked by ## before and after the abstract. Due to space limitations they may be abbreviated. Up to three editors of an anthology will be listed; if there are more, only the first will appear (added by ,*et al.*).

Only those papers in journals will be abstracted that are relevant to cultural/social anthropology - which mainly applies in the case of interdisciplinary, or predominantly sociological journals. *AA* also tries to cover subjects related to, or influencing, anthropology, i.e. if they are relevant for present discourses. Thus, there may be material from history, folklore studies, linguistics, sociology, philosophy, etc., if there is an intersection with present debates in anthropology.

Keywords serve as an "abstract of the abstract" - for a quick assessment of the contents. Page numbers in the Subject Index refer to the page where the *Keywords* listings appear.

Terms of the *Subject Index* – which is identical with the *Keywords* in alphabetical order – do not follow the Thesaurus principle but are chosen rather loosely and generously, according to need, and there is no strict formal rule to limit their number. In many cases, Subject Index terms try to be specific rather than general, in order to reduce the time of searching. Thus, if there is a topic relating to ‚history’, it will be specified like ‚history (Guinea)’, or ‚history and literacy’, so that users do not have to check all ‚history’ entries.

Regarding alphabetical order, the German Umlaut (ä, ö, ü) will be broken up into ae, oe, ue in the text, but is disregarded in the indexes.

The publishers, museums and research institutions must be thanked for their generally prompt deliveries of the books requested for *Anthropological Abstracts*.

And last but not least: many thanks to Veit Hopf (LIT Verlag) for publishing this journal!

PD Dr. Ulrich Oberdiek, *Reader in Anthropology*,
Institut für Ethnologie, Ruprecht-Karls-Universität
Heidelberg, Germany,
and:
Institut für Ethnologie und Afrikanistik (Department f. Kulturwissenschaften u. Altertumskunde),
Ludwig-Maximilians-Universität, München.

Contact:
Quäkerst. 7
79102 Freiburg/Germany
Phone+Fax: Germany: 0761/70 72 344
e-mail: Ulrich.Oberdiek@t-online.de

GENERAL/THEORETICAL/HISTORICAL STUDIES

AMELINA, ANNA
Transnationale Migration jenseits von Assimilation und Akkulturation.
Transnationale Inklusion und hybride Wissensordnungen als konzeptio-
nelle Alternativen zur Assimilations- und Akkulturationsdebatte
Berliner Journal für Soziologie 20.2010:257-279
Keywords: migration, transnational migration, assimilation, acculturation, inclusion, cultural interference

##*Transnational alternatives to migration beyond assimilation and*
acculturation. Transnational inclusion and hybrid cultural orders as
conceptual alternatives to the assimilation and acculturation debate
Classic theories of migration describe international migration as one-way movements and investigate the cultural adjustment of migrants into a "majority society". Contrary to this view, the article raises the question of new, conceptual possibilities to describe migrants' assimilation and acculturation without conceptually focusing on a nation-state frame. In doing so, it makes reference to theories of transnational migration which define migration as a circular process connecting both sending and receiving contexts. This perspective enables, first, to analyze „structural assimilation" as multiple simultaneous inclusions of individuals into societal institutions in different nation-state locations. Secondly, it suggests to consider acculturation as a cultural adjustment of migrants' knowledge patterns, which goes hand in hand with the maintenance of cultural „otherness".##

BALSLEV, ANINDITA & DIRK EVERS (Eds.)
Compassion in the world's religions. Envisioning human solidarity
Berlin: Lit Verlag 2010
175 pp., Euro 19.90; ISBN 3-643-10476-2
Keywords: comparative religion, history of religions, religion and compassion, compassion and religion, Islam, Hinduism, Zoroastrianism, Judaism, solidarity

The papers in this book, written by „scholars from different religious traditions" originate from a meeting New Delhi in 2009 (a program called *Cross-cultural conversation*) to foster inter-religious understanding, similar to the historical example of the „Parliament of World's Religions". At this conference the topic of compassion was central.

SWAMINATHAN, MANKOMBU S.: Concern and Compassion as Pathways to Making Hunger History

DHALLA, HOMI: The Zoroastrian Ethos of Compassion

SAMDHONG, RINPOCHE: On Compassion: The Buddhist Approach

LAKH DOR, GESHE: Compassion – A Complement to Wisdom

SASTRY, KUTUMBA: Compassion: Etymology, Rituals, Anecdotes from the Hindu Tradition

CARROLL, BOB: "Have we not all one Father?" Toward a Psychohistory of the Jewish Idea of Compassion

GOSHEN-GOTTSTEIN, ALON: Compassion – The Teachings of R. Nachman of Breslav

BERNHARDT, REINHOLD: Compassion as a core-element of Christian ethics

ENGINEER, ASGHAR ALI: Compassion in Islam – Theology and History

BALSLEV, ANINDITA N.: Compassion as a Shared Value: Indic Perspectives

CHANDRA, LOKESH: Human Solidarity

EVERS, DIRK: Can Compassion foster Human Solidarity? A Christian Perspective

TOSCANO, ROBERTO: Compassion and solidarity in international relations

GIACOMELLI, GIORGIO: Human Solidarity – A Diplomat's View

BARTH, VOLKER, FRANK HALBACH & BERND HIRSCH (Eds.)
Xenotopien. Verortungen des Fremden im 19. Jahrhundert
(Kulturgeschichtliche Perspektiven 9)
Berlin: Lit Verlag 2010
225 pp., Euro 24.90; ISBN 3-643-10624-7
Keywords: xenotopias, alterity, otherness, Forster, J.R., travelogues, nostalgia, orientalism, colonialism, noble savage, Humboldt, A.v.

Xenotopias. Locating alterity in the 19th century
Xenotopia is understood as analogous to Foucault's concept of heterotopia, as spaces where alterity is produced and stage-setted, which is particularly the case in museums and exhibitions, in the theater and in literature in the 19th century – which is presented to a mass audience. Their effects vary: As spaces of information mediation they aim at integrating alterity into existing patterns of order. But they are contact zones also, creating a framework for intercultural contact. The contributions by specialists of history, theater, dance, anthropology, history of art, literature show that xenotopias are not ‚alien spaces' but spaces of the Other in the self.

SCHNEIDER, UTE: Ins Bild gesetzt: Fremdheit in der Kartographie des 19. Jahrhundert [Put into the picture: Alterity in the cartography of the 19th century]

NUTZ, THOMAS: Logistik der Mobilien: Exotische Artefakte zwischen Zentrum und Peripherie. Das Beispiel Johann Reinhold Forster [Logistics of mobile things: Exotic artifacts between center and periphery. The case of Johann Reinhold Forster]

TORMA, FRANZISKA: Abschied vom Orient? Nostalgie als Aneignungsstrategie Turkestans in Reiseberichten des Fin de siècle [Goodbye to the Orient? Nostalgia as an appropriation strategy of Turkestan in travelogues of the Fin de siècle]

FISCHER, ANNEMARIE: Monumentum und *locus amoenus*: Das Wechselspiel zwischen Architektur und Natur im Bühnenbild zur Zeit der goetheschen Jahrhundertwende [Monumentum and *locus amoenus*: The interplay between architecture and nature in the stage set at the time of Goethe's turn of the century]

HAITZINGER, NICOLE, CLAUDIA JESCHKE & GABI VETTER-MANN: Zwischen Erde und Himmel: *La Périe* und der orientalische Traum [*La Périe* and the oriental dream]

SCHNELL, WERNER: Ein gerissener und wieder verknoteter Traditionsfaden: Dubuffet und die Orientalisten [A torn and re-tied thread of tradition: Dubuffet and the orientalists]

HONOLD, ALEXANDER: Der Zug ins Exotische: Die Eisenbahn im kolonialen Zeitalter [The train to the Exotic: Railway in the colonial age]

HEIDEMANN, FRANK: Die künstlichen Berge: Indische Hill Stations und die Produktion von Edlen Wilden [Artificial hills: Indian Hill Stations and the production of noble savages]

ENGLHART, ANDREAS: Die ‚allgemeine Übersicht' der Erscheinungen im ‚Naturgemälde': Entwürfe eines panoramatischen Raums des Fremden in Alexander von Humboldts *Kosmos* [The ‚general overview' of manifestations in the ‚painting of nature': Blueprints of a panoramic space of the Other in Alexander von Humboldt's *Kosmos*]

MAHLER, ANDREAS: Venedig als Xenotopos in der Literatur des ausgehenden neunzehnten Jahrhunderts [Venice as a xenotopos in the literature of the late 19th century]

BECK, ULRICH & ANGELIKA POFERL (Eds.)
Große Armut, großer Reichtum. Zur Transnationalisierung sozialer Ungleichheit
(Edition Suhrkamp 2614)
Berlin: Suhrkamp Verlag 2010
694 pp., Euro 18,-; ISBN 3-518-12614-1
Keywords: poverty, wealth and poverty, transnational inequality, inequality, migration and poverty, capitalism, national perspective, global perspective

Great poverty, great wealth. On the transnationalization of social inequality
The 22 papers of this reader by international (Wallerstein, Sklair, Sassen, Bhalla, Amartya Sen...) and German (Beck, Stichweh, Poferl, Berking, Römhild) authors (many of them sociologists), discuss this topic of suffering in a global perspective. The papers, empirical studies and theoretical concepts, deal with globalization and exclusion, spatial aspects of inequality, postnational models of membership, global justice, power and status in transnational spaces, migrants as avantgarde, gender and capitalism, risk society, or class analysis. Some argue for giving up the nationally limited perspective to be able to deal with worldwide claims for social participation and human rights.

BEDORF, THOMAS
Verkennende Anerkennung. Über Identität und Politik
(Suhrkamp Taschenbuch Wissenschaft 1930)
Berlin: Suhrkamp Verlag 2010
262 pp., Euro 12,-; ISBN 3-518-29530-4
Keywords: misrecognition, politics and identity, identity, recognition of cultures, cultures and identity, Taylor, C., intercultural recognition, reciprocity

Misrecognizing recognition. On identity and politics
Bedorf discusses three models, or theories, of recognition: intercultural (starting with multicultural diagnosis), intersubjectivist (spheres of interaction, ethics of primary reciprocity, cognitivism), and subjectifying recognition. The first two aims at relations between cultures/subjects, the third focuses on the generation of the subject itself. He further discusses – avoiding essentialism – identity as the integrating *telos* in these models, repeatedly utilizing Charles Taylor's „moral topography of the self". These discussions take place against the background of various minorities striving for recognition, respect and public visibility, and rights. Bedorf opines that there cannot be any „complete" recognition, and that, in processes of mutual recognition, these are necessarily processes of *mis*recognition.

BEETZ, MICHAEL
Das unliebsame System. Herbert Spencers Werk als Prototyp einer Universaltheorie
Zeitschrift für Soziologie 39.2010:22-37
Keywords: Spencer, H., universal theory, social Darwinism, biology, progress

##*The Disagreeable System. Herbert Spencer's Work as a Prototype of Universal Theory*
Unlike Marx, Durkheim, or Weber, sociology's collective memory does not hold Spencer in high esteem. His theory is presumed to propagate social Darwinism; and it seems to presuppose a teleological idea of progress and the acceptance of biological analogies. Less attention is paid to his historical role, his writings, and the cosmological character of his entire work. However, Spencer's philosophical system can be understood as an analytical ontology providing a catalogue of scientific topics. Contrary to monothetic diagnoses and methodological theories, it typifies an altogether different kind of universal theory, of which Luhmann's system theory would later be another instance. Since the work of Spencer marks the most universal and radical version of this theoretical type, to engage with Spencer means to address the issue of the possibility of universal theory and its functional equivalents. Such an engagement may help to make current debates over social theory more precise.##

BELLER, SIEGHARD & ANDREA BENDER
Kognitionsethnologie und Kognitionspsychologie: Synergien nutzen
Zeitschrift für Ethnologie 135.2010:233-248
Keywords: cognitive anthropology, cognitive psychology, research methods, human reasoning, culture and cognition

##*Cognitive anthropology and cognitive psychology: making use of synergies*
Cognitive Anthropology and Cognitive Psychology are both empirical sciences that aim at contributing to a comprehensive picture of human reasoning and action by taking a cognitive perspective on cultural and psychological phenomena. However, the two disciplines take different angles on these topics with respect to content and methods. The position that a stronger integration of the two angles will provide desirable synergy effects is substantiated with regard to three aspects: the different methodologies (field studies vs. experiments), the often observed division of labour (analysis of culture-specific contents vs. analysis of general cognitive processes), and the cultural constitution of cognition. As such synergy effects will not emerge automatically, we discuss some implications for research practice resulting from the goal of a stronger cooperation between the two disciplines, and present some successful projects.##

BENDER, ANDREA & SIEGHARD BELLER
Die Ethnologie - eine tragende Säule im Gebäude der Kognitions- wissenschaften?
Zeitschrift für Ethnologie 135.2010:185-198
Keywords: cognitive sciences, anthropology and cognitive sciences

##*Anthropology - a supporting pillar in the cognitive science edifice?*
Three decades ago, the cognitive sciences were established as the joint effort of six disciplines, united by the common goal of exploring the foundations of human cognition. Based already on twenty years of cognitive work, anthropology had become a supporting pillar in this interdisciplinary edifice that contributed to and benefited from the ongoing exchange of ideas, theoretical concepts, and methods. Since then, however, anthropology's presence and influence has continuously decreased - to the extent that it is now, and particularly so in the German-speaking areas, no longer even recognized as a potential partner in this interdisciplinary

endeavor. This paper aims to make a case for changing this infelicitous situation. It exemplifies why cognitive approaches are still important for anthropology and why anthropology is indispensable for the cognitive sciences; it highlights some of the attempts that have been undertaken recently to improve the relationship; and finally, it tries to demonstrate why engaging in interdisciplinary cooperation is of mutual benefit.##

BENDER, ANDREA & BIRGITT RÖTTGER-RÖSSLER
Ethnologie und Kognitionswissenschaften im Dialog
Zeitschrift für Ethnologie 135.2010:177183
Keywords: cognitivism, anthropology and psychology, cultural patterns, human cognition

Anthropology and cognitive science in dialogue
##Even though anthropology had been one of the pioneers in the foundation of cognitive science, over the last decades a growing alienation between the two disciplines has been undeniable. In their introduction to this *special issue* of *Zeitschrift für Ethnologie*, Andrea Bender and Birgitt Röttger-Rössler argue that this relation should be reconsidered. Anthropology and cognitive science can contribute to each other's research through an emphasis on the interdependency of cultural patterns and human cognition. Scientific collaboration between members of the two fields could not only help explaining gaps in the respective theoretical frameworks but also open up new perspectives for future research.##

BERGER, PETER ET AL. (Eds.)
Feldforschung. Ethnologische Zugänge zu sozialen Wirklichkeiten
Berlin: Weißensee Verlag 2009
(Berliner Beiträge zur Ethnologie 15)
506 pp., Euro 32,-; ISBN 3-89998-114-8
Keywords: fieldwork, difference, friendship, ethics, emotion and fieldwork, Baule, Oromo, conflict, reflexivity, crisis of representation, representation, media, visual anthropology, group fieldwork

Fieldwork. Social realities in anthropological perspectives
##Fieldwork is the sine qua non of socio-cultural anthropology. However, it is neither uncontested nor can its ethical, epistemological and

methodological implications ultimately be delineated, As the practice of fieldwork itself theorizing about it is work in progress in interrelation with new challenges. The fifteen contributions collected here (six of which are in English language) discuss problems of ethics and involvement as well as of emotion and embodiment. They demonstrate the crucial ways cultural, historical and political contingencies of a given field shape the research process and suggest new ways for anthropological field research.##

BERGER, PETER ET AL.: Feldforschung: Berliner Perspektiven auf eine ethnologische Methode [Fieldwork: Berlin perspectives about an anthropological method]

EMDE, SINA: 'Coloured Fields': Some Reflections on Sameness, Difference and Friendship in Anthropological Research

BLINDT, ULRIKE: Die Frage der Einmischung: Moralische Dilemmata im Feld und die Hilflosigkeit der Ethnologen [The question of interference: Moral dilemmas in the field and the helplessness of anthropologists]

DILGER, HANSJÖRG: ETHIK! Oder: Moralische und methodologische Implikationen der Wissensproduktion in einer ethnologischen Feldforschung über „das Unsagbare" [Ethics! Or: moral and methodological implications of knowledge production in anthropological fieldwork about the „Unmentionable"]

BERGER, PETER: Assessing the Relevance and Effects of 'Key Emotional Episodes' for the Fieldwork Process

FUHRMANN, BERIT: 'Ethnography with Tears?': Krankheit und Hexerei als leibliche Erkenntniszugänge [Illness and witchcraft as corporeal approaches to cognition]

BERRENBERG, JEANNE: The Importance of Being Unimportant

LUIG, UTE: Von der Schwierigkeit, Geschichte zu erforschen: Feldforschung unter Baule in der Elfenbeinküste (1974-76) [On the difficulty to research history: Fieldwork among the Baule at the Ivory Coast]

ZITELMANN, THOMAS: Towards the Acquisition of Conflict Knowledge: Fieldwork among the Oromo Liberation Front and Oromo Refugees during the 1980s

PFEFFER, GEORG: Feldforschung: Versuch einer autobiographischen Bilanz [Fieldwork: An autobiographical stock-taking]

HARDENBERG, ROLAND: Geheim, verboten, unrein: Beschreibung einer Feldforschungssituation in Puri (Indien) [Secret, prohibited, impure: Description of a fieldwork situation in Puri, India]

CHAUDHARY, AZAM: Contrasting Reflexive Positionality the German 'Native' Pakistani and the ‚Afar' German fieldworks

MEYER, CHRISTIAN: Ereignisethnographie und methodologischer Situationalismus: Auswege aus der Krise der ethnographischen Repräsentation? [Event ethnography and methodological situationalism: Exits from the crisis of ethnographic representation?]

TRIESELMANN, WERNER: Filmische Inszenierung von Fremdheit als Zugang zur Feldforschung. Ein medienethnologischer Ansatz [Movie stagesetting of alterity as an approach to fieldwork]

REYHE, RUNE & LINUS STROTHMANN: Für eine Methodik des Zu-Zweit-Forschens: Erfahrungsbericht eines Dialogs [For a method of dyadic research: Report on the experience of a dialog]

SUBHA, TANKA B.: Group Fieldwork: Revisiting an Old Anthropological Practice in India

BINAS-PREISENDÖRFER, SUSANNE
Klänge im Zeitalter ihrer medialen Verfügbarkeit. Popmusik auf globalen Märkten in lokalen Kontexten
Bielefeld: Transcript Verlag 2010
277 pp., Euro 27.80; ISBN 3-8376-1459-6

Keywords: pop music, music and markets, local and music, digitization, lullabies, world music, global pop

Sounds in the age of their medial availability. Pop music on global markets in local contexts
Digitization has activated debates on global availability. The free use of cultural achievements and eroding copyright determine the legitimacy of cultural practices, and this pertains especially to music. The author uses the medial journey of a Melanesian lullaby to trace the effects of technical storage, editing, and appropriation in various musico-cultural contexts and segments of the economy of music. The author discusses and analyzes various contemporary phenomena of popular music, especially in the context of globalization, such as the question of homogenization vs. diversification, cultural musical encounters, world music, and factors connected with the media: availability, technical reproduction, and economy.

BLÄTTEL-MINK, BIRGIT & KAI-UWE HELLMANN (Eds.)
Prosumer revisited. Zur Aktualität einer Debatte
Wiesbaden: VS Verlag 2010
232 pp., Euro 29.90; ISBN 3-531-16935-4
Keywords: prosumers, marketers and prosumers, consumers, eBay, cultural goods, freeskiing and consumption, subcultures and consumption, trans-market civilization

Prosumer revisited. On the topicality of a debate
This book is based on a project on consumerism and prosumerism and a conference that took place at the University of Frankfurt in 2009. Some of the papers read there constitute the present book.
HELLMANN, KAI-UWE: Prosumer revisited. Zur Aktualität einer Debatte
KOTLER, PHILIP: The prosumer movement. A new challenge for marketers
RITZER, GEORGE: Focusing on the prosumer. On correcting an error in the history of social theory
BLUTNER, DORIS: Vom Konsumenten zum Prosumenten [From consumer to prosumer]
HANEKOP, HEIDEMARIE & VOLKER WITTKE: Kollaboration der Prosumenten. Die vernachlässigte Dimension des Prosuming-Konzepts [Collaboration of prosumers. The neglected dimension of the prosuming concept]
BLÄTTEL-MINK, BIRGIT: Prosuming im online-gestützten Gebraucht-warenhandel und Nachhaltigkeit. Das Beispiel eBay [Prosuming in online-based second-hand trade and sustainability. The case of eBay]
PANZER, GERHARD: Die Funktion inszenierter Prosumption für Qualität und Wert kultureller Güter [The function of directed prosumption for the quality and value of cultural goods]
MARSCHALL, JÖRG: „So ein Auto ist eigentlich ‚ne lebende Baustelle". Markengemeinschaften als Prosumentenkollektive [Brand communities as prosumer collectives]
WOERMANN, NIKLAS: Subcultures of Prosumption. Differenzierung durch Prosumption in der Freeski-Szene [Qualification through prosumption in the Freeski scene]
BRUNS, AXEL: Vom Prosumenten zum Produtzer [From prosument to produtzer]
VOLKMANN, UTE: Sekundäre Leistungsrolle. Eine differenzierungs-theoretische Einordnung des Prosumenten am Beispiel des „Leser-Reporters" [Secondary role of achievement. A differentiation-theoretical positioning of the prosument in the case of the „reader-reporter"]

BOHLKEN, EIKE & CHRISTIAN THIES (Eds.)
Handbuch Anthropologie. Der Mensch zwischen Natur, Kultur und Technik
Stuttgart: Metzler Verlag 2009
460pp., Euro 49.95; ISBN 3-476-02228-8
Keywords: anthropologists, philosophers

Handbook anthropology. The human being between nature, culture, and technology
This handbook, edited by two philosophers, is organized by first presenting portraits of 15 important thinkers, half of them being philosophers but there are also Marcel Mauss, Lévi-Strauss, Geertz, and Foucault. The second part is organized according to approaches, from behaviorism to sociobiology and behavioral genetics – i.e. very broad categories not identical with cultural/social anthropological approaches proper. The subject section of the book has 41 topics which come closer to cultural/social anthropological perspectives, such as aggression, age, family, identity, power, morals, intoxication, language, sexuality, or *zoon politicon*.

BOURRIER, MATHILDE
Pour une sociologie «embarquée» des univers à risque?
Tsantsa 15.2010:28-37
Keywords: high-risk organizations, risk organizations, organizations of risk, negotiating risky research, embeddedness

For an «embedded» sociology of high-risk organizations
Gaining access to high-risk organizations remains difficult but once achieved working in such an environment does not necessarily compel the researcher to create specific tools and techniques. More thought than is normal for the sociological method per se should, therefore, go into the conditions under which access is negotiated. In this article, we posit that a strategy similar to that adopted in developments in reporting, for this case dubbed «embedded journalism», is taking shape in sociology. Of course, an «embedded sociology» does not yet formally exist. Yet, the way in which sociologists have to approach high-risk environments leads us to apply the metaphor of «embeddedness» and to see the extent to which a comparison might be fruitful. On the one hand the strategy of embeddedness offers avenues for access to the private core of places, rarely

the subject of sociological research. On the other, it compels us to question anew the implications of how such access practices affect sociological production.##

BREUER, STEFAN
Karl Marx als Soziologe
Sociologia Internationalis 48.2010:173-199
Keywords: Marx, K., sociology and Karl Marx, economy and Karl Marx

Karl Marx as a sociologist
##Contemporary German sociology has elevated Marx into the pantheon of its founding fathers. Affiliation with his work is claimed not only for the theory of social stratification, but also for the concepts of social differentiation and indeed of society tout court. This essay weighs the reasons advanced for such treatment, and finds them wanting: in terms of scientific typology, Marx belongs in the lineage of classical political economy, not that of sociology. Nevertheless, his analysis of the capitalist system has sociological relevance, capturing certain facts and processes that must be acknowledged even by a sociology oriented on the subjective understanding of meaning.##

BUNGE, MARIO
Soziale Mechanismen und mechanismische Erklärungen
Berliner Journal für Soziologie 20.2010:371-381
Keywords: social mechanisms, mechanism, mechanismic explanations, social change, Merton, R.K.

Social mechanisms and mechanismic explanation
##Researchers in all fields dealing with reality wish to explain facts once they have described them. The prevailing account of explanation in the philosophical literature is the "covering law model". According to this opinion, to explain a fact is to deduce the proposition(s) describing it from a theory together with the appropriate data, such as initial conditions. This is not how explanation is conceived of in the advanced factual sciences. In these, to explain a fact consists in unveiling the mechanism that makes the thing in question "tick". In turn, a mechanism consists in the process(es) characteristic of the given thing. For example, metabolism is the central

mechanism of living beings, learning is that of schools, and trade that of markets. I call *mechanismic* this kind of explanation. Therefore, anyone wishing to control a concrete system had better start by finding out its typical mechanisms, so as to maintain or alter them. This is what social control mechanisms, from cooperation and charity to legislation and violence, are supposed to accomplish. Typically, social mechanisms involve at least two levels, micro (individual) and macro (institutional). Consequently they can be neither understood nor designed on the basis of either individualism or holism. I argue that only systemism, the view that every thing is either a system or a component of one, can satisfactorily account for the centrality of mechanisms. Warning: Merton, Giddens and others often called "structure" what I call "mechanism". Following mathematical usage, I define the structure of a system as the set of all the relations (in particular cohesive bonds) among the system component (endostructure), as well as the relations between the system components and things in the environment.##

CAMPREGHER, CHRISTOPH
Öko-Apostel, Revolutionäre und Weltverbesserer. Entwicklungszusammenarbeit mit Indigenen
Cargo. Zeitschrift für Ethnologie 30.2010:79-83
Keywords: development, global economy, economy and NGOs, NGOs, equality in development

Ecological adepts, revolutionaries, and starry-eyed idealists. Development cooperation with indigenous peoples
The author discusses the work of NGOs in general (with local cases) and regarding ecology, equality of participation, culture concepts, and altogether recent trends in development cooperation.

CEVOLINI, ALBERTO
Die Einrichtung der Versicherung als soziologisches Problem
Sociologia Internationalis 48.2010:65-90
Keywords: insurance, risk society, time-buying, descisions and insurance

The establishment of insurance as a sociological problem

##Insurance is one of the most discussed but at the same time controversial business institutions of modern society. While studies about the juridical origins and the probability conditions of insurance contracts abound, there is till today only few sociological research trying to include such institution into a general theory of society. This article suggests a searching path whose aim is to couple the problem of insurance to the functional differentiation of modern society and to the achievement of a money-mechanism in an autonomous economical system. Empirical evidences are used, i.e. medieval contracts, diaries, accounting books. The article tries then to explain, how a danger-community changes itself in a risk-society. The thesis arises that insurance institutions do represent a highly improbable way of time-buying and selling, whose business is indispensable for the reproduction of risky decisions.##

CHANIOTIS, ANGELOS ET AL. (Eds.)
Body, Performance, Agency, and Experience. Including an E-Book-Version...
(Ritual dynamics and the science of ritual 2)
Wiesbaden: Harrassowitz 2010
583 pp., Euro 98,-; ISBN 3-447-06202-2
Keywords: ritual, performance and ritual, agency and ritual, funerals, mortuary rituals, Ayahuasca, dance and rituals, shamanism, Buddhism, healing, liturgy

##Held in Heidelberg from September 29 to October 2, 2008 by the collaborative research center SFB 619 "Ritual Dynamics", the international conference "Ritual Dynamics and the Science of Ritual" assembled most of the leading experts on rituals studies and more than 600 participants for the purpose of reassessing the traditional subject in view of the latest research. The results, which are presented in five volumes, are pathbreaking for future transcultural, interdisciplinary and multimethodical research on rituals. The convention was marked by the broad range of disciplines and the corresponding diversity of methods. It embraced a great variety of topics in terms of cultural geography and spanned a time horizon from antiquity to the present. The proceedings show how broadly the term ritual can be defined, as well as the conditions, modes and functions of ritual actions in different cultures of the present and past.##
SANDERSON, ALEXIS: Ritual for Oneself and Ritual for Others
WIDLOK, THOMAS: What is theValue of Rituals? Effects of Complexity in Australian Rituals and Beyond

MEYER, CHRISTIAN: Performing Spirits: Shifting Agencies in Brazilian Umbanda Rituals

WEBER, CLAUDIA: Prescribed Agency - A Contradiction in Terms? Differences between the Tantric *adhikāra* Concept and the Sociological term of Agency

TADDEI, ANDREA: Memory, Performance and Pleasure in Greek Rituals

STROHM, REINHARD: Memories of Ancient Rituals in Early Opera

BELLIA, ANGELA: Music and Rite: Representations of Female Figures of Musicians in Greek Sicily (Sixth-Third Centuries B.C.)

SOAR, KATHRYN: Circular Dance Performance in the Prehistoric Aegean

DUBBINI, RACHELE: *Agones* on the Greek *Agora* between Ritual and Spectacle: Some Examples from the Peloponnese

VENN, EDWARD: Evoking the "Marvellous": Ritual in Michael Tippett's *The Midsummer Marriage*

TONNAER, ANKE: Fear and fascination for a White Maggot: Savouring the Other in Tourist Ritual

STIFOSS-HANSSEN, HANS & LARS J. DANBOLT: The Dead and the Numb Body: Disaster and Ritual Memory

BOLT, SOPHIE & ERIC VENBRUX: Funerals Without a Corpse: Awkwardness in Mortuary Rituals for Body Donors

PEELEN, JANNEKE: Social Birth of Stillborn Children: The Body as Matter, the Body as Person

HEESSELS, MEIKE: From Commercial goods to Cherished Ash Objects: Mediating Contact with the Dead through the Body

WOJTKOWIAK, JOANNA: Living through Ritual in the Face of Death

QUARTIER, THOMAS: "This Is My Body": Physical, spiritual, and social dimensions of embodiment in Roman-Catholic funerals

SAMUEL, GEOFFREY: Inner Work and the Connection between Anthropological and Psychological Analysis

CARDEÑA, ETZEL & WENDY E. COUSINS: From Artifice to Actuality: Ritual, Shamanism, Hypnosis, and Healing

WINKELMAN, MICHAEL: Evolutionary Origins of Human Ritual

JOHNSTON, JAY: Physiognomy of the Invisible: Ritual, Subtle Anatomy, and Ethics

BÖTTGER, DANIEL: Empirical Test of the Effect of Facial Feedback on the Subjective Experience of Ritual

ECHTLER, MAGNUS: A Real Mass Worship they will never Forget: Rituals and Cognition in the Nazareth Baptist Church, South Africa

TURFJELL, DAVID: Ritual, Emotion, and the Navigation of the Self

ODENTHAL, ANDREAS: Ritual Experience: Theology and Psycho-analysis in Dialogue about the Liturgy of the Catholic Church
GERKE, BARBARA: The Multivocality of Ritual Experience: Long-Life Empowerments among Tibetan Communities in the Darjeeling Hills, India
SUMEGI, ANGELA: Being the Deity: The Inner Work of Buddhist and Shamanic Ritual
HAUSER, BEATRIX: Dramatic Changes. The Experience of a Religious Play in the Mega-City of Delhi
EDE, YOLANDA VAN: Differing Roads to Grace: Spanish and Japanese sensory approaches to dance
POOLE, W. GERARD: Emotional Cultivation and the Chaotic Emotion: Towards a Theory of Ritual, Musical, and Emotional Parallel Morphology, as Encountered in Andalusian Ritual Practices
PIKE, SARAH M.: Performing Grief in Formal and Informal Rituals at the Burning Man Festival
WEINHILD, JAN: Navigating the Inner Work: The Experience of Ayahuasca within Santo Daime Rituals

DAUTH, HARIKA
Der Atatürk-Kult. Vom Mythos des türkischen Säkularismus
Cargo. Zeitschrift für Ethnologie 30.2010:69-77
Keywords: Atatürk, K., secularism myth, myth of secularism

The cult of Atatürk. On the myth of Turkish secularism
In this essay Dauth discusses the the myth, and ethnographic-empirical background of the Atatürk cult in general, and in an informed way (based on 14 months of life in Istanbul).

DELLWING, MICHAEL
Rituelle Spiele mit Beziehungen. Goffmans Normen zwischen Interaktionsordnung und ironischer Offenheit
Berliner Journal für Soziologie 20.2010:527-544
Keywords: ritual, Goffman, E., pragmatism, irony, Durkheim, E., order and ritual

##Ritual games of relationship negotiation. Goffman's norms between the interaction order and ironist openness

On the one hand, Erving Goffman's work has been perceived as an explication of the interaction order indebted to Durkheim. On the other hand however, it is known as an ironist rejection of order. Goffman made use of this ambivalence without ever attempting to resolve it. Instead of looking at Goffman as a cartographer of the order of everyday life's order, he can be seen as someone who plays with different perspectives about the everyday game with order. Thus, his Durkheimian part is not order, but ritual, which he transforms into ritual play; norms are then ritual games with relationships.##

DHARAMPAL-FRICK, GITA & ROBERT LANGER ET AL (Eds.)
Transfer and spaces. Including an E-Book-Version...
(Ritual dynamics and the science of ritual 5)
Wiesbaden: Harrassowitz 2010
401 pp., Euro 98,-; ISBN 3-447-06205-3
Keywords: ritual, transfer (ritual), Pentecostalism, shamanism, globalization, Tyva, neo-shamans, hybridity, possession, Sikhs, Pirs, asceticism, OBCs, marriage, Hinduism, pilgrimage, Buddhism, tourism, Alevis, Cem ritual, Easter processions, altars, foundation rituals

##Held in Heidelberg from September 29 to October 2, 2008 by the collaborative research center SFB 619 "Ritual Dynamics", the international conference "Ritual Dynamics and the Science of Ritual" assembled most of the leading experts on rituals studies and more than 600 participants for the purpose of reassessing the traditional subject in view of the latest research. The results, which are presented in five volumes, are pathbreaking for future transcultural, interdisciplinary and multimethodical research on rituals. The convention was marked by the broad range of disciplines and the corresponding diversity of methods. It embraced a great variety of topics in terms of cultural geography and spanned a time horizon from antiquity to the present. The proceedings show how broadly the term ritual can be defined, as well as the conditions, modes and functions of ritual actions in different cultures of the present and past.##
ASTORI, DAVIDE: Passover *seder* and Masonic *agape*: Evidence of (Re)Invention or Transfer of Ritual?
BELCHER, KIMBERLY H.: Ritual Identity and Cultural Transition in the Syro-Malabar Rite Catholic Church in Chicago
CHANNA, SUBHADRA MITRA: Ritual Transfer: From the High to the Low in Hindu-Tibetan Himalayan Communities

FISCHER, MORITZ: "Let the Tears Flow": Performative transfer of healing rituals in Pentecostal healing events between Repetition and Renewal and their Impact on the Globalisation of Christianity

GRÜNWEDEL, HEIKO: Shamanic Rituals from Siberia to Europe: Cultural Exchanges between Indigenous Healing Traditions of the Tyva and Neo-Shamans in Germany

HARMS, ARNE: Happy Mothers, Proud Sons: Hybridity, Possession and a Heterotopy among Guyanese Hindus

KHOKHLOVA, LIUDMILA V.: Ritual Transfer in the History of the Sikh Community: with Special Reference to the Sikh Marriage Ceremony

MOHAMMAD, AFSAR: Following the Pir: Temporary Asceticism and Village Religion in South India

OTTO, PAUL: *Wampum*: The Transfer and Creation of Rituals on the Early American Frontier

PATEL, TULSI: Transformations in Marriage Rituals: The Case of Urbanising OBCs in Rajasthan

SITHARAMAN, SUDHA: Conflict over Worship: A Study of the Sri Guru Dattatreya Swami Bababudhan Dargah in South India

SUTTON, DONALD S.: Transfers of Ritual at a Northern Sichuan Site: Tibetan and Han Chinese Pilgrims, and Han Chinese Tourists

TAŞĞIN, AHMET: The Eastern Church in Sweden: The Transfer of Syrian Orthodox Rituals from Turkey to Europe

YAMAN, ALI: Ritual Transfer within the Anatolian Alevis: A Comparative Approach to the *Cem*-Ritual

MOCKO, ANNE: Rewriting Ritual: Community and Ethnicity in a San Francisco Performance of American Origins

PETERSEN, NILS HOLGER: *Il Doge* and Easter Processions at San Marco in Early Modern Venice

FLEISCHER, JENS: The Cornerstone and Its Ritual Power

JÜRGENSEN, MARTIN WANGSGAARD: In the Sphere of Sacrosanctity: Altars as Generator of space in the Late Middle Age

SCHRAVEN, MINOU: Foundation Rituals in Renaissance Italy: The Case of the Bentivoglio Tower in Bologna

MEYER-DIETRICH, ERIKA: Religion that is Heard in Public spaces: Sound Production in Ancient Egypt in a Ritual Context

JESSEN, MADS DENGSØ: Altars and the Sacred Space: An Investigation into the Missionary Use of Portable Altars

DIECKMANN, BERNHARD, HANS MALMEDE & KATRIN ULLMANN (Eds.)
Identität Bewegung Inszenierung
(Düsseldorfer Schriften zu Kultur und Medien 1)
Frankfurt: Lang Verlag 2010
290 pp., Euro 54.80; ISBN 3-631-59457-5
Keywords: stage-management, motion, mediality, Semprún, J., photography, memory and body, hybridity, neuronal resonance, cinéma beur, Almodovar, P., gender, performativity

Identity Motion Stage-management
DIECKMANN, BERNHARD, HANS MALMEDE & KATRIN ULLMANN: Identität - Bewegung – Inszenierung [Identity, motion, stage-management]
BORSÒ, VITTORIA: Materialität, Medialität und Immanenz: Wider die Medialität als Drittes [Materiality, mediality, and immanence: Against mediality as a third]
MAEDER, DOMINIK: Zwischen Eingedenken und Unvergesslichem. Erinnerungsformen in den Romanen Jorge Semprúns [Between remembrance and the unforgettable. Forms of remembering in the novels of J. Semprún]
HERGET, THOMAS: Photographisches Gedächtnis. Zur Konstruktion der Erinnerung im Medium der Photographie [Photographic memory. On the construction of memory in the medium of photography]
RIEGEL, DAGNY: Trauma über den Tod hinaus. Das Verhältnis von Gedächtnis zu Körper und Raum am Beispiel von MEMENTO und ANDERLAND [A trauma beyond death. The relation of memory and body and space in MEMENTO und ANDERLAND]
ROCHOLL, MARIUS: Intermediales Erzählen in Pedro Almodovars LA MALA EDUCACION – SCHLECHTE ERZIEHUNG [Intermedial narrative in Almodovars LA MALA EDUCACION]
BLUM, CLAUDIA: Der hybride Raum als neue Weltordnung? Identität im „cinéma beur" [Hybrid space as new world order? Identity in the „cinéma beur"]
ULLMANN, KATRIN: „Sometimes I feel more Morocco than French." Selbstverortungen junger Europäer in der Gegenwart [Self-positioning of present young Europeans]
KEMPMANN, MICHAEL: Neuronale Resonanz und Habitus: Über Verhältnisse zwischen neuro- und kulturwissenschaftlichen Kommunikationsmodellen [Neuronal resonance and habitus: On relations between neuro and cultural-scientific models of communication]

TRINKAUS, STEPHAN: Mit der Arbeit aufhören – Spiel, Objekt-beziehung und Medialität [Quitting labor – Play, object relations, and mediality]

FRANK, FRANZ: Unscharfe Sektoren – Beobachtungen zum kinemato-graphischen Raum [Blurred sectors – Observations on kinematographic space]

KLON, BENJAMIN-LEW: Im Spiegelkabinett des Wong Kar-Wai [In the room of distorting mirrors of Wong Kar-Wai]

MÄCHTEL, ALEXANDRA: Der Laser, das unerforschte Medium in der Medienwissenschaft [Laser – the ‚un-researched' medium in media science]

BEßLICH, HOLGER: Die Wiederkehr des Gleichen? Über die (Un-) Wiederholbarkeit im Fußball [The return of the same? On the irretrievableness in soccer/football]

SKRANDIES, TIMO: Ästhetische Räume, künstlerische Strategien und die Politik der Kunst. Das Beispiel Gregor Schneider [Aesthetic spaces, artistic strategies and the politics of art]

VOLLMER, MAIKE: Noch nicht Bild - Zur Funktion der Performativität im zeitgenössischen Tanz [On the function of performativity in contemporary dance]

GELDMACHER, PAMELA: Eine performative Suche nach (Auf-) Brüchen der Geschlechterordnung [A performative search for breaks/ breaking-ups of the gender order]

KÜHN, GREGOR: Cross-Dressing und das dritte Geschlecht [Cross-dressing and the third gender]

COBAN, KORAY: Anarchy in the media?

GREGOR, CHRISTINA: Eine Kontroverse um den Begriff Public Diplomacy und die Methoden der strategischen Vermarktung US-amerikanischer Außenpolitik [A controversy on the notion of public diplomacy and the methods of strategic marketing of US-American foreign policy]

DIEDRICH, MARIA I. & JÜRGEN HEINRICHS (Eds.)
From black to Schwarz. Cultural crossovers between African America and Germany
(Forecast. Forum for European contributions to African American studies 18)
Berlin: Lit Verlag, Michigan State University Press 2010
388 pp., Euro 39.90; ISBN 3-643-10109-9

Keywords: cultural exchange, exchange of cultures, colonial art, Locke, A., Askari, Krenek, E., Jazz, Williams, J.A., Fassbinder, R.W., cinema, diaspora, gender, Reiss, W., Brandenburg, M., Patterson, B.

##*From black to Schwarz* explores the long and varied history of the exchanges between African America and Germany with a particular focus on cultural interplay. Covering a wide range of media of expression – music, performance, film, scholarship, literature, visual arts, reviews – the essays collected in this volume trace and analyze cultural interaction, collaboration and mutual transformation that began in the 18th century, literally boomed during the Harlem Renaissance/Weimar Republic, could not even be liquidated by the Third Reich's ‚Degenerate Art' campaigns, and, with new media available to further exchanges, is still increasingly empowering and inspiring participants on both sides of the Atlantic.##

WALLINGER, HANNA: The Africanist presence in 19th-century German writers

SCHWARZ, A.B. CHRISTA: New Negro Renaissance – ‚Neger-Renaissance': crossovers between African American and Germany during the era of the Harlem Renaissance

SCHNECK, PETER: The Askari as New Negro: Alain Locke and German colonial art

ROGOWSKI, CHRISTIAN: Staging the African American conquest of Old Europe: Ernst Krenek's *Jonny spielt auf*

WIPPLINGER, JONATHAN: Bridging the Great divides: Cultural difference and transnationalism at Frankfurt's *Jazzklasse*

CAMPT, TINA M.: Pictures of „US"? Blackness, diaspora and the Afro-German subject

GRAML, GUNDOLF: Black bodies on white snow: The reconstruction of Germanness as White in Luis Trenker's *Der verlorene Sohn* (The prodigal son) (1934)

OPPEL, CHRISTINA: (Re)writing twentieth-century slavery: John A. Williams' *Clifford's Blues* as neo-slave narrative

REID, MARK: Reading *Clifford's Blues* and Blacks in Nazi Germany in PostNegritude time

FENNER, ANGELICA: The rebirth of the nation: Cinematic discourses of race and reconstruction in transnational perspective

LAWS, PAGE R.: Rainer and *Der weiße Neger*: Fassbinder's and Kaufmann's on and off screen affair as German racial allegory

WRIGHT, MICHELLE M.: In a nation or diaspora? Gender, sexuality and Afro-German subject formation

RITTELMANN, LEESA: Winold Reiss to Kara Walker: The silhouette in Black American art

HEINRICHS, JÜRGEN: Mixed media, mixed identities: The universal aesthetics of Marc Brandenburg

CASSEL OLIVER, VALERIE: On Ben Patterson: „I'm glad you asked me that question"

BOYD, MELBA JOYCE: Poetry, Jazz and the politics of aesthetics: Transcontinental connections between German ,68ers and African American culture

DIMLER-WITTLEDER, PETRA
Trauern in Gemeinschaft. Eine Ethnographie des Trauerns
(Interethnische Beziehungen und Kulturwandel 69)
Berlin: Lit Verlag 2010
298 pp., Euro 29.90; ISBN 3-643-10642-1
Keywords: mourning, ethnography of mourning, death and mourning, comfort in mourning

Mourning in community. An ethnography of mourning
This book deals with death and mourning in a German cultural setting, and specifically with groups who have been formed for that purpose. So the author discusses cultures and contexts of death and mourning from within, because she herself has been a mourner. Her argument is that being a member of such groups is a pre-condition for assessing them in an adequate way. She discusses central categories of this complex (death, the corpse, the ritual, the tabu) and authors (e.g., Freud, K. Abraham, Melanie Klein, Y. Spiegel, La Planche), phases and symptoms of mourning, and she has used various sources for her study, such as letters, journals, interviews with undertakers and mourning persons. The next part is devoted to processes taking place in mourning groups and types of groups, and finally various ways and contents of mourning in the groups are presented.

DOHRMANN, ALKE, DIRK BUSTORF & NICOLE POISSONNIER (Eds.)
Schweifgebiete. Festschrift für Ulrich Braukämper
(Ethnologie 37)
Berlin: Lit Verlag 2010
346 pp., 34.90; ISBN 3-643-10209-6

Keywords: festschrift U. Braukämper, Braukämper, U., meritocracy, Dullay, killing, peace ceremony, body, oral tradition, wedding, Bayansi, spirits, Selt'é, pastoralism, dignitaries, ethnicity, Banabans, labor division, Hadiyya, calendars, environment, myths, biography, fieldwork, museums, Iron Age

Areas of roaming. Festschrift for Ulrich Braukämper
The papers in this festschrift, the 65th birthday of U. Braukämper, discuss current topics of the anthropology of religion, economy, politics, museal anthropology, fieldwork, and archaeology and history. The main regional focus is Ethiopia, but other African, Asian and South American countries, are represented, too.
STRECK, BERNHARD: Bedarfsarbeit – Faulheit und Fleiß außerhalb der Leistungsgesellschaft [Necessary work. Laziness and industry outside of an achievement-oriented society]
AMBORN, HERMANN: Gada – Spurensuche bei den Dullay (Südwest-äthiopien) [Gada – Searching for traces among the Dullay, Southwest Ethiopia]
POISSONNIER, NICOLE: Killing – a Rite of Passage?
STRECKER, IVO: Vicissitudes of Cultural Contact. Notes on the Background of a Peace Ceremony at Arbore
DAMMERS, KIM: Gestures and Body Language Used in Public Greetings and Departures in Addis Ababa
HORSTMANN, CATHRIN: Some Notes on Hadiyya Oral Traditions
AL-ERYANI, SUSANNE: Alte Bräuche in neuen Räumen. Von Hochzeitsfeierlichkeiten in Ṣanᶜā', Republik Jemen [Old customs in new spaces. On wedding celebrations in Ṣanᶜā', Republic of Yemen]
THIEL, JOSEF F.: Wiedergeboren in den Enkeln. Alternierende Beziehungen der Bayansi/Demokratische Republik Kongo [Born again in grandchildren. Alternating relations of the Bayansi, Democratic Republic of Congo]
SMIDT, WOLBERT: Erd-, Baum- und Wassergeister in Tigray und Eritrea. Religiöse Konzepte jenseits des Christentums [Earth, tree, and water spirits in Tigray and Eritrea. Religious concepts beyond Christianity]
BUSTORF, DIRK: Schicksal. Fluch und Segen in der Ätiologie der mündlichen Geschichte. Das Beispiel der Selt'é (Athiopien) [Fate. Curse

and blessing in the etiology of oral history. The case of the Selt'é, Ethiopia]

STRIEDTER, KARL HEINZ: Elemente eines prähistorischen Pastoralismus in der Zentralsahara [Elements of a prehistorical pastoralism in the Central Sahara]

PLATTE, EDITHA: Würdenträgerinnen in muslimischen Kleinkönigtümern Nordnigerias [Female dignitaries in Muslim little kingdoms of Northern Nigeria]

WAGNER, EWALD: Harariner Richter [Judges of Harar]

FUCHS, PETER: Die Ethnisierung nationaler politischer Konflikte im Tschad und in Darfur (Sudan) [The ethnicization of national political conflicts in the Tchad and Darfur, Sudan]

HERMANN, ELFRIEDE: Ethnizität als transformierbare Ressource. Formung und Gebrauch von ethnischer Identität bei den Banabans [Ethnicity as a transformable resource. Formation and use of ethnic identity among the Banabans]

HESSE, KLAUS: Die Mongolei und China. Spezialisierung, Arbeitsteilung, Politik und Formen des Austausches in historisch-ethnologischer Perspektive [Mongolia and China. Specialization, division of labor, politics and forms of exchange in historical-anthropological perspective]

DOHRMANN, ALKE: Conflicts on Land in the Southern Highlands of Ethiopia. A Case Study on the Hadiyya People

KIRSCHT, HOLGER: 28 „Months" Make one Year. An Agricultural Calendar in Bomo State, Nigeria

MAASS, PETRA: All lies in the eye of the beholder. Anthropological Perspectives on Cultural Landscapcs, Religious Worldviews and Environmental Conservation

MÜNZEL, MARK: Gekreuzte Mythen. Die Ungewissheit der Feldforschung am Beispiel eines frühen Vorläufer [Crossed myths. The uncertainty of fieldwork in the case of an early forerunner]

TAFLA, BAIRU: The Reminiscence Dimension of Historiography. The State o Biographical Writing in Ethiopia and Eritrea

GASCON, ALAIN: Ethiopia in 1936. Adventurers Rather than Ethnologists

DAAIMO, SOLOMOON: Some Memories of My Life as a Research Assistant

DEIMEL, CLAUS: Reise zu den Hadiyya in Qaalisha bei Hossana, über Addis Abeba, mit Wendo Genet und Shashemene [Voyage to the Hadiyya in Qaalisha near Hossana, via Addis Ababa, with Wendo Genet and Shashemene]

HAUSER-SCHÄUBLIN, BRIGITTA: Jenseits von Feldforschung. Kooperationen mit Partnern in den Ländern unserer Untersuchungen [Beyond fieldwork. Cooperation with partners in the countries of our research]
STEIN, LOTHAR: Das wechselvolle Schicksal des Ethnographischen Museums in Khartoum [The varied fate of the Ethnographic museum in Khartoum]
KRÜGER, GUNDOLF: Von Macao nach Göttingen und zurück. Ein Südsee-Gemälde im interkulturellen Dialog [From Macao to Göttingen and back. A South Seas painting in intercultural dialog]
LIESEGANG, GERHARD: Selma (8th Century BC), Takusheyi (13th/14th Century AD) and Surame (16th/17th Century AD). Research on the rise of the Iron Age, the States of Kalsina, Gobir and Kebbi
BUSTORF, DIRK: Ausgewählte Bibliographie Ulrich Braukämpers [Select bibliography of Ulrich Braukämper]

DRESSLER, ANGELA
Nah dran und live dabei. Kollaboration und verdeckte Autorschaft in der Auslandsberichterstattung
Tsantsa 15.2010:18-27
Keywords: hidden authorship, authorship, news reporting, journalism, fieldwork and journalism, nation state

##Close up - Collaboration and Hidden Authorship in Foreign News Reporting
This article examines journalistic practice in foreign news reporting. Although its journalistic practice may raise a variety of questions similar to those brought up by ethnographic fieldwork, the author demonstrates how journalism is bound to an event-focused timeframe as well as to-specific socio-political conditions. From this perspective, the article discusses the obligations news reporting has to the nation-state as well as the much neglected collaboration of correspondents within local networks.##

ECKHARD, PETRA, MICHAEL FUCHS & WALTER W. HÖLBLING
(Eds.)
Landscapes of postmodernity. Concepts and paradigms of critical theory
(American studies in Austria 10)
Wien: Lit Verlag 2010
286 pp., Euro 29.90; ISBN 3-643-50201-8
Keywords: postmodernism, identity and postmodernism, literature and postmodernism

##In *Landscapes of postmodernity*, a group of young scholars link key concepts of postmodern thought to our present everyday experience in which we change our identities on a regular basis. While many of the essays look at less conventional modes of aesthetic representation – computer games, graphic novels, telenovelas, queer and animated films – others analyze more canonical works following less conventional approaches. Either way, the cultural and literary cartographies presented in this book allow America to be conceived as polymorphous or transnational, celebrating a new American self that is aware and proud of its non-Anglo-Saxon origins.## Many of the 17 papers analyze literary texts, but there are also discussions of a more anthropological kind, e.g. the discussion of Derrida's reading of Lévi-Strauss.

EGLI, WERNER M. & LUCIA KERSTEN (Eds.)
Kindheit und Jugend anderswo. Ergebnisse ethnographischer Feld-forschungen
(Ethnologie. Forschung und Wissenschaft 22)
Wien: Lit Verlag 2010
298 pp., Euro 31.90; ISBN 3-643-80044-2
Keywords: childhood (anthropology of), anthropology of childhood, Mbyá-Guaraní, Roma, Tsiggani, Tamilian youths

Childhood and youth elsewhere. Results of ethnographic fieldwork
These papers by final-year students of the University of Zurich, based on participant observation, share the perspective of recent approaches of the anthropology of childhood considering the child as an independent social actor.
EGLI, WERNER M.: Neue Kindheitsforschung, teilnehmende Beob-achtung und fremde Lebenswelten von Kindern und Jugendlichen
BARRERA-WILLI, SERAINA PEÑA: Freiheit und Kontrolle des *pochy* – Kindheit und Adoleszenz bei den Mbyá-Guaraní in Argentinien

LEGNINI, PATRIZIA: *Die Roma haben ein Kilogramm Gold, wir Zigeuner nur ein Viertelgramm* – Ethnische Zugehörigkeit im Alltag von Romakindern eines rumänischen Dorfes
ZEHNDER-MALCOTSIS, SOFIA: Was bedeutet die Alphabetisierung der Kinder der Tsiggani in Ano Liosia, Athen?
LÜTHI, CHRISTINA: Westafrikanische Traditionen der Oralliteratur im städtischen Kontext: Funktionen der Märchen im Alltag von Kindern in Bamako, Mali
HUBER, ROSMARIE: Arbeit oder Schule? – Der Kreislauf von Kinderarbeit in der Textilstadt Tirupur, Südindien
FREI, SARAH: ...weil sie nicht meine Schwester ist! – Heimalltag und Familienbild in zwei Mädchenheimen in Bolivien
GÄUMANN, SIMONE: Perspektiven von paraguayanischen Jugendlichen in *villas miserias* in Buenos Aires im Spannungsfeld des argentinischen Migrationsdiskurses
KERSTEN, LUCIA: Entre le voile et la mini-jupe – Wie Jugendliche maghrebinischer Herkunft in der Banlieue von Paris Lebensweise und Identität aushandeln
HALFHIDE, THERESE: Der Freitag ist mein Lieblingstag - Aufwachsen als tamilisches Mädchen im Schweizer Exil
EMCH, SYLVIA EILEEN & URSINA MÜLLER: Einblick in den Alltag von tamilischen Jugendlichen in der Schweiz als Grundlage eines interkulturellen Lehrmittels

ENGLHART, ANDREAS, ANNEMARIE FISCHER & KATERINA GEHL (Eds.)
Die Öffentlichkeit des Fremden. Inszenierungen kultureller Alterität im langen 19. Jahrhundert
(Kulturgeschichtliche Perspektiven 7)
Berlin: Lit Verlag 2010
276 pp., Euro 29.90; ISBN 3-643-10568-4
Keywords: alterity, stagesetting alterity, identity, colonialism, slavery, orientalism, Pavlova, A., censorship, theater satire

The public sphere of the Other. Productions of cultural alterity in the long 19th century
BALME, CHRISTOPHER: Pan-Polynesian identity and the colonial public sphere: The New Zealand International Exhibition, Christchurch 1906-07

MAY, YOMB: Der „Orient... im Auge meiner Tochter des Okzidents..." Ida von Hahn-Hahn und die (De-)Konstruktion kultureller Alterität in den *Orientalischen Briefen* [Ida von Hahn-Hahn and the (De-)Construction of cultural alterity in the *Orientalische Briefe*]

LUKANITSCHEWA, SWETLANA: Die Fremdheit als Schlüssel zum Erfolg. Russische Dandys – Schöpfer und Protagonisten des Mythos „Silbernes Zeitalter" [Alterity as a key to success. Russian dandies – creators and protagonists of the myth of the „Silver Age"]

HAITZINGER, NICOLE: Anna Pawlova: „à travers les siècles". Zu Kreation, Rezeption und Re-Konstruktion eines Personalstils [On the creation, reception, and re-construction of a personal style]

STAUSS, SEBASTIAN: Die Fremdheit des Obszönen. Zur Zensur im Münchener Theaterleben um 1900 [The alterity of the obscene. On censorship in theaters in Munich around 1900]

ENGLHART, ANDREAS: Die Theatralität des öffentlichen Skandals um Karl Boromäus Alexander Sessas Theaterstück *Unser Verkehr* [The theatrality of the public scandal on K.B.A. Sessa's play *Unser Verkehr*]

DOBREVA, DOROTEJA: Historisches Gedächtnis und Identitätskonstruktionen im bulgarischen Europäisierungsdiskurs. Das Fallbeispiel „Batak" [Historical memory and identity constructions in the Bulgarian Europeization discourse – The case of „Batak"]

FISCHER, ANNEMARIE: Die Dramaturgie des Skandals. Therese Krones und der Raubmörder Severin von Jaroszinky als Bühnenfiguren [The dramaturgy of the scandal. Therese Krones and the robber and murderer Severin von Jaroszinky as stage figures]

PARGNER, BIRGIT: Die Persiflierung der Öffentlichkeit und des Fremden in der Theatersatire Ludwig Tiecks [The ,satirization' of the public and the Other in the theater satire of Ludwig Tieck]

GEHL, KATERINA & PETAR PETROV: Die „deutschen" Journalisten oder wie Gustav Freytag auf die bulgarische Öffentlichkeit traf [The ,German' journalists, or, how Gustav Freytag encountered the Bulgarian public]

OTTENBACHER, ALBERT: Das öffentliche Bild des Indianers. Eine kleine Genealogie eines auch heute noch virulenten medialen Images [The public image of the American Indian. A little genealogy of a still virulent medial image]

RIESCHE, BARBARA: „Frohe Aussichten" für die „Africanische Hundsgesichte". Die europäische Sklavereidebatte in der deutschen Öffentlichkeit [„Happy prospects" for the „African miserables". The European debate on slavery in the German public]

DRÜNER, ANNIE-LAURE: Eher „feig" als „tapfer"? Neue Dokumente zur Wiener Staatsoper unter Direktor Erwin Kerber 1936-1940 [New documents on the Vienna State Opera under the director Erwin Kerber 1936-1940]
VETTERMANN, GABI: „... la voix du peuple a dit qui." [The voice of the people has said ‚yes']

ERNST, WALTRAUD (Ed.)
Geschlecht und Innovation. Gender-mainstreaming im Techno-Wissenschaftsbetrieb. Internationale Frauen- und Genderforschung in Niedersachsen. Teilband 4
(Focus Gender 12)
Berlin: Lit Verlag 2010
243 pp., Euro 24.90; ISBN 3-643-10712-1
Keywords: gender-mainstreaming, technology and gender, universities and gender, innovation and gender

Gender and innovation. Gender-mainstreaming in the field of techno-science. International gender research in Lower Saxony [Germany]. Part 4
This volume presents innovative methods of Gender-mainstreaming in higher education institutions, focus are impulses of gender and diversity management the fields of technology and the natural sciences. The culture of science seems to be a challenge in order to continuously create new concepts and strategies for establishing equal opportunities. Why is this so difficult especially in a field which has innovation, in technology and science, as its hallmark? The authors ask questions – to overcome gender hierarchies in the innovation areas of new technologies, IT, physics, robotics, webdesign, and new relationships of technology and gender are designed and discussed.

ERNST, WALTRAUD (Ed.)
Grenzregime. Geschlechterkonstellationen zwischen Kulturen und Räumen der Globalisierung. Internationale Frauen- und Genderforschung in Niedersachsen. Teilband 5
(Focus Gender 13)
Berlin: Lit Verlag 2010
230 pp., Euro 19.90; ISBN 3-643-10713-8
Keywords: gender, globalization and gender, norms of gender

Orders of border. Gender constellations between cultures and spaces of globalization. International gender research in Lower Saxony [Germany]. Part 5
The authors inquire into the intercultural dimension of gender constructs and the history of gender and migration: How, across borders, the understanding of gender has changed just as the persons, moving between cultures and spaces of globalization. Have old hierarchies been abandoned or have they become stronger? How do gender relations change in foreign environments? Are there global transformations of gender relations? The authors analyze old and new, ‚eastern' and ‚western' norms of masculinity. Artistic imagination intertwined with cultural ideologies and political reality become comprehensible. New geographies of gender are generated and researched.

ERNST, WALTRAUD (Ed.)
Ethik – Geschlecht – Medizin. Körpergeschichten in politischer Reflexion. Internationale Frauen- und Genderforschung in Niedersachsen. Teilband 6
(Focus Gender 14)
Berlin: Lit Verlag 2010
210 pp., Euro 19.90; ISBN 3-643-10714-5
Keywords: gender and medicine, medicine and gender, discourses on gender, biotechnology and gender

Ethics – gender – medicine. Body narratives in political reflection. International gender research in Lower Saxony [Germany]. Part 6
The authors inquire into the normative dimension of medical and biological research and the foundation of gender norms through medicine, biology, and ethics. What are the gender-political dimensions of breast cancer research, ovular donation or osteoporosis? What are ideas of gender connected with medical care? Is there a new normative process of gender-

bodies found in present biotechnology? What does it mean when ethics is taken to be a pathway to the liberation from biologistic norms? Old and new narratives of the relations between reproduction, gender, sexuality, health and political rights are discussed. The authors show that these fields of discourse are politically contested. The body, which is to be optimized, is economically focused in such discourses.

EßLINGER, EVA ET AL. (Eds.)
Die Figur des Dritten. Ein kulturwissenschaftliches Paradigma
(Suhrkamp Taschenbuch Wissenschaft 1971)
Berlin: Suhrkamp Verlag 2010
328 pp., Euro 13,-; ISBN 3-518-29571-7
Keywords: third person, tricksters, rivals, parasites, gender, cyborgs, hybridity

The figure of the third. A paradigm of the cultural sciences
The 21 papers in this book deal with key figures of 20th century theorizing on this topic: parasites, tricksters, rivals, third gender, cyborgs, etc. It is argued that this is theoretically significant: categories such as third space or hybridity would show a new sensibility for delimiting and discrimination, whereas before such entities led a shadowy existence in discourses.

FÖRSTER, LARISSA
Nichts gewagt, nichts gewonnen. Die Ausstellung „Anders zur Welt kommen. Das Humboldt-Forum im Schloss. Ein Werkstattblick"
Paideuma 56.2010:241-262
Keywords: museology, exhibitions

Nothing ventured, nothing gained. The exhibition „Anders zur Welt kommen. Das Humboldt-Forum im Schloss. Ein Werkstattblick"
This paper discusses the museal strategy and pedagogics of the Berlin exhibition named in the title. Förster analyzes the new presentation, subdivided in anthropological, cultural-scientific, and museological frames, to ask what the actual program or aim of the exhibition is.

GOTTOWIK, VOLKER (Ed.)
Die Ethnographen des letzten Paradieses
Bielefeld: Transcript Verlag 2010
359 pp., 1 CD, Euro 36.80; ISBN 3-8376-1332-2
Keywords: paradise, Plessen, V.v., Spies, W., cannibals, headhunters, Calonarang, film, Butoh, Artaud, A., orientalism, dance, ritual, music

Ethnographers of the last paradise
The papers of this book are based on a symposium at the University of Frankfurt, Germany, in 2006.
BÖRSCH, DANIEL: Maler, Ethnograph, Ornithologe, Filmemacher und Schriftsteller: Aus dem Leben des Baron Victor von Plessen [Painter, ethnographer, ornithologist, filmmaker and writer. About the life of Baron Victor von Plessen]
PLESSEN, BARON VICTOR VON: Malaiisches Tagebuch. Auszüge aus dem unveröffentlichten Manuskript [Malayan diary. Excerpts from the unpublished manuscript]
SCHLEIERMACHER, STEFFEN: Hommage à Walter Spies
JORDT, HORST: Zeugnisse einer Freundschaft zwischen Spies und von Plessen. Ein Blick in unveröffentlichte Briefe [Evidence of a friendship between Spies and von Plessen. Examples from unpublished letters]
GOTTOWIK, VOLKER: Ein Ritual ohne Höhepunkt? Der Kreis um Walter Spies und die Deutung des *Calonarang* [A ritual without culmination? The circle around Walter Spies and the interpretation of the *Calonarang*]
FUHRMANN, WOLFGANG: Optische Gemälde: Vorläufige Überlegungen zur Geschichte und Ästhetik des ethnographischen Films [Optical paintings. Preliminary reflections on the history and aesthetics of ethnographic film]
WAZ, GERLINDE: Zwischen Ethnographie und Poesie: Victor von Plessens „Südseefilme" im Spiegel seiner Zeit [Between ethnography and poetry: Victor von Plessen's „South sea films" in the mirror of his time]
HORNBACHER, ANNETTE: „Ein Zustand vor der Sprache". Artauds experimentelles Theater als transkultureller Entwurf zwischen balinesischem Tanzdrama und japanischem *Butoh* [„A state before speech". Artaud's experimental theater as transcultural outline between Balinese dance drama and Japanese *Butoh*]
DRESSEL, GERHARD: Plessen Factory. Visuelle Anthropologie und multimediales Theater [Plessen Factory. Visual anthropology and mulitmedial theater]
ZIEGLER, SUSANNE: Mit dem Phonographen unterwegs: Historische Tonaufnahmen indonesischer Musik im Berliner Phonogramm-Archiv [On

the road with the phonograph. Historical recordings of Indonesian music in the Berlin Phonogram Archive]
KRAUS, WERNER: Benevolenter Orientalismus? Linda Bandaras Bemühen um die javanische Musik [Benevolent Orientalism? Linda Bandara's efforts regarding Javanese music]
STEPPUTAT, KENDRA: The Genesis of a Dance-Genre: Walter Spies and the *Kecak*
LANG, DIRK: Von eigenen und fremden Kannibalen: Imagination und Projektion am Beispiel des Kannibalismus-Topos bei den Batak auf Sumatra [Of own and alien cannibals: Imagination and projection in the case of the cannibalism topos among the Batak of Sumatra]
CORDES, HILTRUD: Die Enkel der Kopfjäger. Zur Entstehungsgeschichte eines Dokumentarfilms [The grandchildren of the headhunters. On the making of a documentary]

GRABENHEINRICH, MIRIAM
Ethnologie und Journalismus: Moralischer Kompromiss oder hilfreiche Synergie?
Tsantsa 15.2010:61-71
Keywords: anthropology and journalism, journalism, morals and journalism, media and anthropology

##Anthropology and journalism: moral compromise or useful synergy?
The article examines the insufficient presence of German ethnologists in the media. The author describes her own work experience as a TV-journalist focusing on reports about emigrants and foreign cultures - within Germany and abroad. The systematization of her practical experience allows the author to demonstrate where a need for an ethnoloqical point of view exists in journalism and how ethnologists could maintain a continuous and meaningful presence in the media.##

HAHN, ALOIS
Körper und Gedächtnis
Wiesbaden: VS Verlag 2010
245 pp., Euro 24.95; ISBN 3-531-16924-8
Keywords: memory and body, body and memory, tattoo, confession, rites, secular rites, habitus, performance

41

Body and memory
All mental abilities have an organic basis – this is the connection between memory and body. As a social fact recollection needs repeated „incantations" so it does not disappear. Individual memory and personal recollection is often connected with conscious processes, but frequently certain experiences of learning have become unconscious mental and bodily moulding. Hahn systematically focuses on this connection between body and memory, dealing with the „stagesetting of memory", cultic and secular rites and ceremonies, attention, habitus and memory, handwriting and tattoo, the „honesty" of the body, identifications and their social construction, the complex of confessions, culture as a medium, bourgeois culture as education, and the sociology of the bricoleur.

HASSE, RAIMUND & LUCIA SCHMIDT
Unternehmertum, Arbeit, Sprache. Zur Mikrofundierung des Neo-Institutionalismus
Sociologia Internationalis 48.2010:1-28
Keywords: entrepreneurship, work, language, neo-institutionalism, institutionalism

Entrepreneurship, work, language. On the micro-foundation of neo-institutionalism
##This article discusses concepts of a micro-foundation of the new institutionalism stemming from the idea of institutlonal entrepreneurs which intentionally utilize and shape institutions. The sociology of social problems serves as a frame of reference and as a conceptual resource pool. Based on conceptual linkages between the new institutionalism and the sociology of social problems we develop two suggestions for advancing the micro-perspective of the new institutionalism: (1) a revision of the concept of work in order to better incorporate mundane local practices and routinized behaviour, and (2) a linguistic turn which instead of focusing on rhetorical strategies - highlights the everyday handling of accounts.##

HEINTEL, PETER & LARISSA KRAINER
Geschichtlich-Kulturelle Nachhaltigkeit
Erwägen Wissen Ethik 21.2010:435-449
Keywords: sustainability, culture and sustainability, self-reflection

Historical-cultural sustainability
##Peter Heintel and Larissa Krainer propose to free the term sustainability of its moral meaning (content, implications) and to analyse it as a cultural concept. To do so, culture should not be seen as an extension of the classic three-pillar mode of sustainability, but as a moment in which new meaning is created. In a second step, culture is shown to be a dialectical phenomenon and a term of process. If sustainability is to have an effect, it is necessary to design, define and collectively agree on a new aim for history, the authors Peter Heintel and Larissa Krainer argue. After a detailed criticism of the "Modell Neuzeit" – which they demonstrate is one-sided (and unbalanced) – Heintel and Krainer propose to design cultural sustainability as a culture of self-reflection.##

HEINTZ, BETTINA
Numerische Differenz. Überlegungen zu einer Soziologie des (quantita-tiven) Vergleichs
Zeitschrift für Soziologie 39.2010:162-181
Keywords: quantitative comparison, comparison in sociology, numerical difference, difference and quantification

##Numerical Difference. Toward a Sociology of (Quantitative) comparisons
In this contribution comparisons are considered to be elementary social forms, and they are analyzed within a communication-theoretical perspective. Across different media of communication, comparisons are expressed linguistically, numerically, or visually, and this differentiation is the focus of the present investigation. The use of numbers, visual representations, and language each affects communication in a particular manner, and quantification is particularly effective in promoting the acceptance of communication. This effectiveness corresponds to what is here termed the „numerical difference," a difference illustrated by the ubiquitous use of quantitative comparisons drawn from statistics, rankings, or ratings. In the first part of the paper elementary characterlstics of comparisons and their communicativeness are discussed. In the second part, the differentiation of linguistic, visual, and numerical media is utilized in order to investigate how the form of messages may influence the likelihood of their acceptance. These observations are related to issues of globalization in the third part of the paper, where they are discussed with

respect to concepts employed by studies of diffusion within the new institutionalism.##

HEPP, ANDREAS, MARCO HÖHN & WALDEMAR VOGELSANG (Eds.)
Populäre Events. Medienevents, Spielevents, Spaßevents. 2. Überarbeitete Auflage
Wiesbaden: VS Verlag 2010
318 pp., Euro 34.95; ISBN 3-531-15770-2
Keywords: events, media events, game events, fun events, trekkies, communication, cyber games, Halloween

Popular events. Media events, game events, fun events. 2nd edition
HEPP, ANDREAS: Stefan Raab, Regina Zindler und der Maschen-drahtzaun: Ein populäres Medienereignis als Beispiel der Eventisierung von Medienkommunikation [Stefan Raab, Regina Zindler and the wire netting-fence: A popular media event as a case of eventization of media communication]
EISENBÜRGER, IRIS: Stars, Sterne und unendliche Weiten: die Events der Trekkie-Szene [STARS, stars and infinite space: The events of the Trekki scene]
HEPP, ANDREAS & VERONIKA KRÖNERT: Der katholische Welt-jugendtag als Hybridevent: Religiöse Medienereignisse im Spannungsfeld zwischen Mediatisierung und Individualisierung [The Catholic World Youth Meeting as hybrid event: Religious media events between mediatization and individualization]
VOGELSANG, WALDEMAR: LAN-Partys: die Eventisierung eines jugendkulturellen Erlebnisraums [LAN parties: The eventization of a youth-cultural space of experience]
WIMMER, JEFFREY et al.: „Beyond the game"?! Die World Cyber Games 2008 in Köln als populäres Spielevent der Computerspielindustrie [The World Cyber Games 2008 in Cologne as a popular game event of the computer game industry]
LORIG, PHILIPP & WALDEMAR VOGELSANG: Paintball: Sport oder Kriegsspiel? – Räuber und Gendarm als Event für Erwachsene [Paintball: Sports or war game? Cops and robbers as events for adults]
HÖHN, MARCO: Tot aber glücklich. Halloween – die Nacht der lebenden Toten als Event-Mix [Dead but happy. Halloween – the night of the living dead as event mix]

KRÜDENER, BETTINA & JÖRGEN SCHULZE-KRÜDENER: Da war noch was: Zur Eventisierung des Jugendbrauchtums in der Region am Beispiel der Spaßfeten [There was something else: on the eventization of youth traditions in a region: The case of fun parties]

HILLEBRANDT, FRANK
Modernität - zur Kritik eines Schlüsselbegriffs soziologischer Zeitdiagnose
Berliner Journal für Soziologie 20.2010:153-178
Keywords: modernity, Weber, M.

##*Modernity: A critique of a key concept in the sociological diagnosis of our time*
The article discusses different research perspectives of the concept of modernity. Against the background of Max Weber's diagnosis of the time, it analyzes the circular construction of this concept. Using discourse theory, the article traces the most important meanings of this concept as developed in the work of authors like Beck, Luhmann, Taylor, Habermas and Eisenstadt. Contrary to existing assumptions of a universal concept of modernity, the article argues for a sociological analysis of the concept of modernity in the line of post-colonial approach, which then can be used for a more adequate diagnosis of the time.##

IMBUSCH, PETER (Ed.)
Jugendliche als Täter und Opfer von Gewalt
Wiesbaden: VS Verlag 2010
294 pp., Euro 34.90; ISBN 3-531-17056-5
Keywords: violence, youth violence, victims, culprits, Amok, shootings, gangs

Young people as culprits and victims of violence
IMBUSCH, PETER: Jugendgewalt in Entwicklungsländern – Hintergründe und Erklärungsmuster [Youth violence in developing countries: Background and patterns of explanation]
OLDENBURG, SILKE: Zwischen Akzeptanz und Widerstand – Jugendliche Lebenswelten im kolumbianischen Bürgerkrieg [Between acceptance and resistance: Young life worlds in the Columbian civil war]
KIRSCHNER, ANDREA: Jugend, Gewalt und sozialer Wandel in Afrika [Youth, violence and social change in Africa]

KURTENBACH, SABINE: Jugendliche in Nachkriegsgesellschaften – Kontinuität und Wandel von Gewalt [Young people in postwar societies – Continuity and change of violence]

HUHN, SEBASTIAN, ANNIKA OETTLER & PETER PEETZ: Jugendbanden in Zentralamerika – Zur sozialen Konstruktion einer teuflischen Tätergruppe [Youth gangs in Central America. On the social construction of a devilish group of delinquents]

HEWERA, BIRTE: School shootings und Amok – Perspektiven der Gewaltforschung [School shootings and Amok. Perspectives of violence research]

IRRGANG, BERNHARD
Technik, Ethik, Wissenschaft: Grundlagenreflexionen zur neuen Philosophie der Wissenschaften
Erwägen Wissen Ethik 21.2010:513-523
Keywords: philosophy of science, ethics and science

Technology, ethics, science: Basic reflections on the new philosophy of the sciences
##To reflect the relation between Science and Ethics, I draw on the new wave of philosophy of science and technology, which occured since the l0th century. This new wave reconstructs the identification of complex developmental dynamics in the field of technology, economy, and science, cultural and social embedding. Furthermore it points to the proper place of ethical reflection in this process. Ethics will become a mode of applied philosophy in an external and internal manner. To overcome the Theory of the two cultures I propose a trichotomy of the term science: I) instrumental science of nature and technology, 2) pragmatic cultural studies and social sciences, moral philosophy, 3) theoretical-methodological basic research, ethics. The second distinction: 1) instrumental-technical, 2) institutional social and 3) methodologically justifying level. This differentiation applies to science of nature, science of technology, social sciences und cultural studies and the science of science alike.##

JEBENS, HOLGER
The crisis of anthropology
Paideuma 56.2010:99-121
Keywords: crisis of anthropology, representation

This paper gives a historical overview of major developments or courses anthropology took in the 20th century, subdivided in several phases. ##If the present state of anthropology is to be judged according to what eminent practitioners of the discipline have to say about it, one cannot help having the impression that it is in serious crisis or even faces imminent decline.##

JOHLER, REINHARD, CHRISTIAN MARCHETTI & MONIQUE SCHEER (Eds.)
Doing anthropology in wartime and war zones. World War I and the cultural sciences in Europe
Bielefeld: Transcript Verlag 2010
392 pp., Euro 38.80; ISBN 3-8376-1422-0
Keywords: war zones, prisoners of war, ‚race', World War I, anthropology of war, borders, film

##World War I marks a well-known turning point in anthropology, and this volume is the first to examine the variety of forms it took in Europe. Distinct national traditions emerged and institutes were founded, partly due to collaborations with the military. Researchers in the cultural sciences used war zones to gain access to „informants": prisoner-of-war and refugee camps, occupied territories, even the front lines. Anthropologists tailored their inquiries to aid the war effort, contributed to interpretations of the war as a „struggle" between „races", and assessed the „warlike" nature of the Balkan region, whose crises were key to the outbreak of the Great War.##
SCHEER, MONIQUE, CHRISTIAN MARCHETTI & REINHARD JOHLER: „A Time Like No Other": The Impact of the Great War on European Anthropology
KUKLICK, HENRIKA: Continuity and Change in British Anthropology, 1914-1919
MOGILNER, MARINA: Doing Anthropology in Russian Military Uniform
SIMONIS, PAOLO DE & FABIO DIE: Wartime Folklore: Italian Anthropology and the First World War

EVANS, ANDREW D.: Science behind the Lines: The effects of World War I on Anthropology in Germany
JOHLER, REINHARD: Laboratory Conditions: German-Speaking Volkskunde and the Great War
PROMITZER, CHRISTIAN: „Betwixt and Between": Physical Anthropology in Bulgaria and Serbia until the End of the First World War
CORDILEONE, DIANA REYNOLDS: Swords into Souvenirs: Bosnian Arts and Crafts under Habsburg Administration
REBER, URSULA: The Experience of Borders: Montenegrin Tribesmen at War
MARCHETTI, CHRISTIAN: Austro-Hungarian *Volkskunde* at War: Scientists on Ethnographic Mission in World War I
BERNER, MARGIT: Large-Scale Anthropological Surveys in Austria-Hungary, 1871-1918
OLIN, MARGARET: Jews among the Peoples: Visual Archives in German Prison Camps during the Great War
SCHEER, MONIQUE: Captive Voices: Phonographic Recordings in the German and Austrian Prisoner-of-War Camps of World War I
LANGE, BRITTA: AfterMath: Anthropological Data from Prisoner-of-War Camps
FUHRMANN, WOLFGANG: Ethnographic Films from Prisoner-of-War Camps and the Aesthetics of Early Cinema

JONG, JOOP DE
Hundertfünfzig Jahre Psychopathologie und Kultur: Von den minderwertigen Frontallappen der Eingeborenen zur kulturellen Neurowissenschaft
Curare 33,1/2.2010:33-41
Keywords: neurosciences, culture and neuroscience, psychopathology, traumatic stress disorder, nature and nurture

The Perennial Debate on Culture and Psychopathology: From Inferior Frontal Lobes to Cultural Neuroscience

A core issue in working with immigrants and refugees – both in the so-called western as well as in the international context of mental health is the relation between biology and culture. This article distinguishes four perspectives of psychopathology that prevailed over the past 150 years. The first perspective is the "dichotomous perspective" that focused on either biology or culture as an explanatory model. This perspective was dominant during colonial times and was partially substituted by and overlapped with the next perspective. The second perspective is the "continuum-perspective" that attributed a "disorder" to the biological, socio-cultural, cognitive, emotional and linguistic aspects of behaviour. The third perspective is the "spectrum-perspective" that filters psychopathology through a prism into divergent behavioural patterns that can be studied. The fourth, which is also the latest and perspective that bears overlaps with the other ones, is the "cultural neuroscientific perspective." Cultural neuroscience tries to answer two main questions: 1) how do cultural traits (e.g., values, beliefs, practices) shape neurobiology (e.g., genetic and neural processes) and behaviour; and 2) how do neurobiological mechanisms (e.g., genetic and neural processes) facilitate the emergence and transmission of cultural traits? This article concludes with an example of traumatic stress disorder showing how cultural neuroscience may help to transcend the dichotomy between universalism and relativism, between nature and nurture, and between genotype and phenotype.##

KAHL, ANTJE
Der Niedergang der klinischen Sektion: Dysfunktionalität der Praxis statt Tabuisierung des toten Körpers
Sociologia Internationalis 48.2010:247-272
Keywords: death, body and death, dissection, autopsy

The decline of clinical dissection/autopsy: Dysfunction of practice instead of tabuization of the dead body
##Despite the fact that the benefits of hospital autopsies are regularly emphasized in medical journals, autopsy rates continue to fall in Germany as well as in other western countries. Therefore explanations for this decline were sought. It was found that the attitudes of the public are surprisingly positive and cannot explain declining autopsy rates. Rather are institutional causes and medical changes of importance. Hospitals, autopsies' vague status as a medical practice seems to be the most relevant factor for their decline.##

KITTS, MARGO ET AL. (Eds.)
State, power, and violence. Including an E-Book-Version...
(Ritual dynamics and the science of ritual 3)
Wiesbaden: Harrassowitz 2010
831 pp., Euro 118,-; ISBN 3-447-06203-9

Keywords: ritual, power and ritual, violence and ritual, Bible and ritual, violence and Bible, empowerment, torture and Abu Ghraib, Abu Ghraib, Tamil resistence, martyrs, sacrifice, kingship, sanctity, propaganda, mediation and ritual, prodigies, corruption, legitimacy, usurpation and ritual, excommunication, academic ritual, Buddhism and ritual, Dussehra rituals

##Held in Heidelberg from September 29 to October 2, 2008 by the collaborative research center SFB 619 "Ritual Dynamics", the international conference "Ritual Dynamics and the Science of Ritual" assembled most of the leading experts on rituals studies and more than 600 participants for the purpose of reassessing the traditional subject in view of the latest research. The results, which are presented in five volumes, are pathbreaking for future transcultural, interdisciplinary and multimethodical research on rituals. The convention was marked by the broad range of disciplines and the corresponding diversity of methods. It embraced a great variety of topics in terms of cultural geography and spanned a time horizon from antiquity to the present. The proceedings show how broadly the term ritual can be defined, as well as the conditions, modes and functions of ritual actions in different cultures of the present and past.##

KITTS, MARGO: Poinē as a Ritual Leitmotif in the Iliad
NOEGEL, SCOTT: The Ritual Use of Linguistic and Textual Violence in the Hebrew Bible and Ancient Near East
WHITAKER, JARROD L.: Empowering Men Ritually in Ancient India
SCHALK, PETER: Memorialisation of Martyrs in the Tamil̠ Resistance Movement of Īl̠am/Lam̐kā
BINDER, WERNER: Ritual Dynamics and Torture: The Performance of Violence and Humiliation at the Abu Ghraib Prison
ARGENTI, ALEXANDRA: The Fear of the Sorcerer: Finding a Peaceful moment for a Sacrifice in Southern Sri Lanka
VORLÄNDER, HANS: Verfassungen und Ritual ein Vormoderne und Moderne
BUC, PHILIPPE: Religion, Coercion, and Violence in Medieval Ritual
FALKOWSKI, WOJCIECH: The Humility and Humiliation of the King – Rituals and Emotions
SPANOS, APOSTOLOS: Imperial Sanctity and Politico-Ecclesiastical Propaganda in Byzantium (Ninth-Fifteenth Century)

QUACK, JOACHIM FRIEDRICH: Political rituals: Sense and Nonsense of a Term and its Application to Ancient Egypt

NUFFELEN, PETER VAN: Beyond Bureaucracy: Ritual Mediation in Late Antiquity

ROSENBERGER, VEIT: Strange Signs, Divine Wrath, and the Dynamics of Rituals: The Expiation of Prodigies in the Roman Republic

TÖBELMANN, PAUL: The Limits of Ritual: Mistakes and Misconceptions, lies and Betrayals at Peace Conferences in Fifteenth Century France

SEELE, PETER: Is There an Economic Benefit in Participating in Rituals? An Institutional Economics Analysis of Transaction Costs and Institutional stability

SCHLÄPPI, DANIEL: Politische Riten. Ämterkauf und geschmierte Plebiszite: Ritualisierler Ressourcentransfer in der Alten Eidgenossenschaft (17. und 18.J ahrhundert) [Political rites. Purchase of offices and corrupt plebiscites: Ritualized resource transfer in the old Swiss Confederation, 17the and 18th centuries]

TORRE, ANGELO: Ritual and Jurisdiction in Northern ltaly (Seventeenth and Eighteenth Centuries

SCHWEDLER, GERALD & ELENI TOUNTA: Usurping Rituals: The Correlation between Formalised Repetitive Behaviour and Legitimacy

SCHWEDLER, GERALD: Usurpation: Term and Concept. A Missing Entry in the "Geschichtliche Grundbegriffe"

DE BACKER, FABRICE: Fragmentation of the Enemy in the Ancient Near East during the Neo-Assyrian Period

GOLDBECK, FABIAN & PATRIZIA ARENA: *Salutationes* in Republican and Imperial Rome: Development, Functions and Usurpations of the Ritual

TOUNTA, ELENI: Usurpation, Acceptance and Legitimacy in Medieval Europe: An Analysis of the Dynamic Relations between Ritual Structure and Political Power

GRESSER, GEORG: Usurping Space Usurping Ritual: Early Medieval Synods in Comparison

KAMP, HERRMANN: New Masters and Old Rituals: Edward I, Robert the Bruce, Philip the Fair and the Role of Rituals in Conquest

JASER, CHRISTIAN: Usurping the Spiritual Sword: Performative and Literary Alienations of Ritual Excommunication

DARTMANN, CHRISTOPH: The Usurpator in the City: Rituals of Power in Northern ltalian City-States

FÜSSEL, MARIAN: Rituals in Crisis? The Dynamics of German Academic Ritual in the Age of Enlightenment

RICHTER, SUSAN: The Prussian Royal Coronation An Usurpation of Ceremonial?

ARENDES, CORD: Rituals in Twentieth-Century Dictatorships: Jean-Bédel Bokassa and "his" Central African Empire, 1976-1919

KULKE, HERMANN: Ritual Sovereignty and Ritual Policy: Some Historiographic Reflections

CHATTOPADHYAYA, B.D.: Festivals as Ritual: An exploration into the convergence of rituals and the state in Early India

FRASCH, TILMAN: Buddha's Tooth Relic: Contesting Rituals and the Early State in Sri Lanka

SAHU, BHAIRABI PRASAD: Rituals, royalty and *Rajya* in early medieval Eastern India

TEUSCHER, ULRIKE: Creating Ritual Structure for a Kingdom: The Case of Medieval Mewar

DEVRA, G.S.L.: Evolution of Antagonistic Rituals in Pre-modern Societies in Asia: A Case Study of Śaka and Jāuhar

NANDA, CHANDI PRASAD: Rethinking "Politico-Ritual states": Sitting on the Lap of a Bhuiyan: Coronation Ceremonies in Keonjhar

PATI, BISWAMOY: The Diverse implications of Legitimacy: Rituals, State and the Common People in Colonial Orissa, 1800-1940s

FRENZ, MARGRET: Mahabali Returns to Kerala: Rituals of Sovereignty in Past and Present

SKODA, UWE: State Rituals after the Abolition of the State: Dossehra Rituals in Bonai/Orissa before and after Merger

KOHL, KARL-HEINZ
The end of anthropology – an endless debate
Paideuma 56.2010:87-98
Keywords: end of anthropology, crisis of representation, writing culture, representation, othering

Kohl contemplates the issue by (among other things) referring to and describing positions of some of the other authors in this volume of Paideuma, as well as positions of authors not represented here. In general, he opines that:
##The current crisis in anthropology thus has little to do with its object of study, which has always been engaged in processes change, but rather with the discipline itself. Following the so-called ‚writing culture debate’, anthropology's customary approaches and forms of representation have

been subjected to a trenchant critique that destabilized the field's very foundations. What we have come to refer to as ‚othering' today is viewed as the field's grate fall from grace. With their critiques of their predecessors' authoritative styles, today's anthropologists have also undermined their own authority. The postcolonial debate has contributed further to anthropology's disempowerment.##

KRAEMER, KLAUS
Propheten der Finanzmärkte. Zur Rolle charismatischer Ideen im Börsengeschehen
Berliner Journal für Soziologie 20.2010:499-526
Keywords: stock markets, ‚prophets' and stock exchange, charisma and economy, Weber, M., expectations and economy

##*Prophets of financial markets. On the role of charismatic ideas in the functioning of stock markets*
Financial markets are marked by considerable uncertainty. Actors in financial markets are nevertheless constantly forced to make decisions. This article pursues the question of how they cope with this problem of decision-making. Based on a critical discussion of the concept of „expectations of expectations", Max Weber's concept of charisma is introduced to gain a better understanding of the influence of „stock market prophets" on investment decisions and to explain such influence as a social process.##

KRAMER, FRITZ W.
Unter Ethnologen und Künstlern
Paideuma 56.2010:7-22
Keywords: Kramer F.W., anthropologists

Among anthropologists and artists
In this account Kramer describes his life and pathway as an anthropologist, which includes reflections on the discipline of anthropology.

KRAY, THORN R.
Metapher und sozialwissenschaftliche Terminologie. Anmerkungen zur räumlichen Metaphorik bei Bruno Latour
Sociologia Internationalis 48.2010:113-142
Keywords: metaphor, Latour, B., Actor-Network-Theory, ANT, rhetoric, hybrid terminology, cognitive linguistics

Metaphor and terminology in the social sciences. Remarks on spatial metaphor in Bruno Latour
##This article examines the conceptual and non-conceptual tools used by a specific social theory to describe our social reality. It argues that the Actor-Network-Theory (ANT) uses the rhetoric figure of metaphor in combination with defined concepts in order to create a hybrid terminology. I will therefore show in some detail what ramifications follow from combining figural speech and concept and how this effects the ANT-architecture. Bringing concept and metaphor together on an operational level of description widens our scientific scope and enriches our perspective on social phenomena. Starting from the point of cognitive linguistics, the article discusses the peculiarities of metaphor and its problematic status in the scientific discourse. After some more general discussion of theories of metaphor, the text focuses on Bruno Latour's book "Reassembling the Social". Latour's (rather unconscious) use of them might be a first step in making metaphor become a helpful element of the account of social practices. Taking the next step, it all boils down to the conclusion that contemporary social theory needs a new kind of symmetry between concept and metaphor in order to heighten its meta-theoretical self-awareness as well as to improve the usefulness of its theoretical tools.##

KREIDE-DAMANI, INGRID (Ed.)
Ethnologie im Nationalsozialismus. Julius Lips und die Geschichte der „Völkerkunde". Mit Beiträgen von Andre Gingrich, Volker Harms, Lydia Icke-Schwalbe, Ingrid Kreide-Damani, Wolfgang Liedtke, Gudrun Meier, Udo Mischek und Dietrich Treide
Wiesbaden: Reichert Verlag 2010
439 pp., Euro 59,-; ISBN 3-89500-774-3
Keywords: Lips, J., National Socialism, Nazism, anthropology and Nazism, racial politics

Anthropology during National Socialism. Julius Lips and the history of „Völkerkunde"
This is a biography on the work of the anthropologist Julius Lips, with special focus on the factor of National Socialism. It provides knowledge and material that has been lacking so far, considering the fact that historical studies of anthropology in the era of Nazism started only in the late 1980s. Thus, the time between 1920 and into the 1960s is dealt with, describing the organizational development of the discipline, nationally and internationally, including the policy of the Hitler regime regarding the sciences, culture, and racial politics, which includes antedecents in the Weimar Republic and repercussions in the two Germanys after World War II.

KUHN, OLIVER
Spekulative Kommunikation und ihre Stigmatisierung - am Beispiel der Verschwörungstheorien. Ein Beitrag zur Soziologie des Nichtwissens
Zeitschrift für Soziologie 39.2010:106-123
Keywords: speculative communication, stigmatization, conspiracy theories, sociology of ignorance, sociology of knowledge, constructionism

##Speculative Communication and its Stigmatization. The Case of Conspiracy Theories. A Contribution to the Sociology of Ignorance
Wrong or speculative "conspiracy theories" provide investigations within the sociology of knowledge with an important example of stigmatized knowledge. The proposition to interpret "speculation" as a third value that subverts the strictly binary (true/false) code of truth opens a theoretical framework for the analysis of the underlying process of stigmatization, claiming that the logical value of speculative statements is indeterminable. This characterization corresponds to a deep ambivalence: in contrast to proven falsity, speculation can maintain the hope of becoming true, but it stands in contrast to the established truth from which it diverges. The sociology of knowledge would profit from an analysis of the communicative conflicts about the conjectural limits of knowledge because these conflicts allow the study of the repression and marginalization of erroneous statements, which are involved in the production of knowledge of all sorts. The justification for this marginalization and exclusion is typically based on ontological arguments which describe methods of testing as external to the construction of knowledge. This presumption is revised by the constructionist perspective offered in this paper, and

"empirical testing" is understood as a form of self-confirmation immanent within the process of the construction of knowledge.##

LEMPERT, WOLFGANG
Soziologische Aufklärung als moralische Passion: Pierre Bourdieu. Versuch der Verführung zu einer provozierenden Lektüre
Wiesbaden: VS Verlag 2010
316 pp., Euro 29,95; ISBN 3-531-17383-2
Keywords: Bourdieu, P., morality and sociology, social research and politics

Sociological enlightenment as moral passion: Pierre Bourdieu. Seducing to read his provocative texts
The author introduces Bourdieu's texts, their intellectual background, and the drives and ambitions, like the integration of morality and economy, behind Bourdieu's writings. He stresses the fact that Bourdieu's research is morally relevant and implies political consequences for justice, dignity of man etc., and Lempert inquires into Bourdieu's identity, the facets of the intellectual, the tireless researcher and so on. The book includes suggestions for reading and research desiderata.

LINDEMANN, GESA
Die Emergenzfunktion des Dritten - ihre Bedeutung für die Analyse der Ordnung einer funktional differenzierten Gesellschaft
Zeitschrift für Soziologie 39.2010:493-511
Keywords: emergence of order, third actor, functional differentiation, Simmel, G., dyadic sociality, order, social order, contingency, alter and ego, ego and alter, action theory, triadic relations

##The Emergence of Order - the Function of the Third Actor and its Relevance for the Analysis of Functional Differentiation
Dyadic notions of sociality are often used as basic concepts for understanding social relations and the emergence of social order. Although Simmel had already introduced the notion of the third actor in addition to the dyad, the systematic relevance of the third actor for social theory has remained unclear. One reason for this is that dyadic concepts of sociality are consistently coupled with the problem of double contingency between Ego and Alter. The third actor, Tertius, becomes a necessary consideration

only once the elementary understanding of the problem of social order is extended. This extension is brought about by complementing the question how the problem of double contingency is solved with the question as to which entities will consider one another as Alter Ego respectively. Following Plessner's theory of the shared world, the second problem is described here as the "problem of contingency of the shared world". The solution of the latter problem defines which entities confront one another in relations of double contingency. In this perspective concrete actions and communications are treated as solutions to two basic problems: the problem of contingency of the shared world and the problem of double contingency between actors. With reference to these elementary problems this contribution offers a revised concept of functional differentiation as an alternative to traditional approaches in systems and action theory. Functionally differentiated realms of society, in this perspective, can be described as being accomplished in and through triadic relations structured in patterns specific to particular functional realms. This idea is explored by discussing science, the economy and law/politics as examples.##

LÜDDEMANN, STEFAN
Kultur. Eine Einführung
Wiesbaden: VS Verlag 2010
122 pp., Euro 14.90; ISBN 3-531-15927-0
Keywords: culture, memory and innovation, meaning, constructivism

Culture. An introduction
Lüddemann presents culture as „a complex system of self-determined ascriptions of meaning" and he sees culture as a dynamic process of the production of meaning that generates necessary guidelines of orientation in modern, functionally complex societies. In such a culture the stabilizing function of memory is connected with innovation which organizes self-images of a society permanently constructing its reality anew. Lüddemann describes how such a society works, having mediality, reflexivity, and heterogeneity as intrinsic characteristics.

LUDWIG, RALPH & DOROTHEE RÖSEBERG (Eds.)
Tout-monde: Interkulturalität, Hybridisierung, Kreolisierung. Kommunikations- und gesellschaftstheoretische Modelle zwischen „alten" und „neuen" Räumen
(Sprache – Identität – Kultur 8)
Frankfurt/M.: Lang Verlag 2010
282 pp. Euro 54.80; ISBN 3-631-59168-0
Keywords: Glissant, E., interculturality, hybridization, creolization, communication models, cultural contact, Rap

Tout-monde: Interculturality, hybridization, creolization. Models of communication and social theory between „old" and „new" spaces
According to the editors the world today is increasingly coined by exchange processes between the ‚old' and ‚new' world, or the ‚third' world, and the authors use Glissant's notion of „Tout-monde", the „all-world" to deal with this complexity of ‚interculturality'.
LUDWIG, RALPH & DOROTHEE RÖSEBERG: Tout-monde: Interkulturalität, Hybridisierung, Kreolisierung. Kommunikations- und gesellschaftstheoretische Modelle zwischen „alten" und „neuen" Räumen [Tout-monde: Interculturality, hybridization, creolization. Models of communication and social theory between „old" and „new" spaces]
RÖSEBERG, DOROTHEE: Interkulturalitätskonzepte in Europa: Versuch einer Zwischenbilanz [Concepts of interculturality in Europe: A provisional appraisal]
FEBEL, GISELA: Von Victor Segalen zu Édouard Glissant: Überlegungen zu einer Poetik des Diversen [From V. Segalen to E. Glissant: Reflections on a poetics of the diverse]
GUGENBERGER, EVA: Das Konzept der Hybridität in der Migrationslinguistik [The concept of hybridity in migration linguistics]
LUDWIG, RALPH: Kreolisierung - ein entgrenzter Begriff? [Creolization – an unlimited term?]
PAGEL, STEVE: Von *Rapa Nui* zur *Isla de Pascua* und zurück: Sprachliche Akkulturation und Distinktion auf der Osterinsel [Linguistic acculturation and distinction on the Easter Island]
ANDRADI, ESTHER: Babel como bendición: La escritura entre los mundos [Literature between the worlds]
BREMER, THOMAS: *Zona crónica*: Der *Nuevo periodismo* und der literarische *blog* in Lateinamerika nach 2000 [The *Nuevo periodismo* and the literary *blog* in Latin America after 2000]
MÜLLER, GESINE: "Au lieu d'obélisques, il a ses palmiers": Kulturkontakte zwischen alten und neuen Räumen. Literarische Momentaufnahmen

der französischen und spanischen Karibik im 19. Jahrhundert [Cultural contact between old and new spaces. Literary snapshots of the French and Spanish Caribbean in the 19th century]

BRÜNING, ANGELA: Creolisation and its Limits in Contemporary Anglophone and Francophone Caribbean Discourse and Fiction

STEMMLER, SUSANNE: Flamenco-Rap: Ein *Tout-Monde* des Klangs [Flamenco Rap. A tout-monde of sound]

GYSSELS, KATHLEEN: Du *Discours antillais* au *Tout-Monde*: Le (c)entrisme d'Edouard Glissant [The centrism of Edouard Glissant]

ENNIS, JUAN A. & STEFAN PFÄNDER: Zur – fragwürdigen – Legitimation des Laboratoriums Kreol(istik) [On the – questionable – legitimation of the laboratory Creol(istics)]

LUIG, UTE
Über das Erinnern von Gewalt und die Verarbeitung des Schmerzes am Beispiel von Flüchtlingen und Ex-Kämpferinnen der TPLF
Curare 33,1/2.2010:60-71
Keywords: memorizing violence, violence, pain, refugees, female ex-fighters, TPLF, war zones, trauma, Scarry, E.

##Memorizing Violence and Coping with Pain: A Study of Refugees and Female Ex-fighters of TPLF in Several Different War Zones
This paper analyzes the interrelations between memory, violence and pain using several different case studies of refugees from Sudan, Chechenya, Somalia, and Cambodia. In addition, we analyze the case of female ex-flghters from the Ethiopian liberation movement TPLF. Our central questions concern the concepts and metaphors, which are used by the refugees and activists to express and remember experiences of violence. In this context, we discuss earlier concepts in the sociology of violence to assess their usefulness. Moreover, we examine Scarry's thesis (1992) that physical pain resists language. Specifically, we explore under which conditions this assumption can be refuted (or not). Finally, the "trauma" concept in these contexts is examined, taking into account that silence or speaking up can be a strategic choice in traumatic situations. In particular, we ask whether trauma remains an adequate concept understanding the complex experiences of violence and pain, and look at possible consequences of the trauma concept for identity constructions.##

MAASER, JOHANNES
*A way of life aus der Sicht Pierre Bourdieus. Der Skinheadstil als Gegen-
stück und Rückgewinnung der Gemeinschaft*
Cargo. Zeitschrift für Ethnologie 30.2010:21-30
Keywords: lifestyle, skinheads, Bourdieu, P., communication of values, values, working class, class values

A way of life seen from Pierre Bourdieu's perspective
Maaser discusses aspects of skinhead subculture and marginalization against the background of mainstream culture, skinheads preserving their specific value orientation through their behavior and lifestyle, and he interprets their aesthetical expression with Bourdieu.

MACKERT, JÜRGEN
Opportunitätsstrukturen und Lebenschancen
Berliner Journal für Soziologie 20.2010:401-420
Keywords: opportunity structures, life-chances, Weber, M., Merton, R., conflict, social conflict, monopolizing resources, closure, social closure

##Opportunity structures and life-chances
The article discusses the development, meaning and theoretical context of both Robert Merton's concept of "opportunity structure" and the concept of "life-chances" that he took up from Max Weber. In order to analyze crucial social conflicts, I argue that both concepts should follow along the lines of conflict theory. While they converge in terms of meaning, we need different theoretical strategies to make their analytical and explanatory power explicit. First, a reinterpretation of the concept of opportunity structure shows that social actors might reduce others' access to options while realizing their own aims; second, life-chances should be put again in a Weberian perspective for two reasons. On the one hand Weber already conceptualizes them in the context of social struggles, on the other hand he shows that the mechanism of social closure helps to understand how people exclude others from life-chances by monopolizing resources.##

MARTTILA, TOMAS
Constrained constructivism in post-structural discourse analysis
Sociologia Internationalis 48.2010:91-112
Keywords: constructivism, constrained constructivism, epistemology, research strategies, Diaz-Bone, R., cognition

##The post-structural notion of the transitivity of knowledge implicates that empirical discourse analysis is involved in co-constructing of the reality it observes. In order to remain consistent with the acclaimed transitient nature of knowledge, discourse analysts should ensure that the discursive orders they observe are in line with their own discursivity. This article locates the possibility to assess the co-construction of social reality in the methodological position of constrained constructivism. Drawing on the French epistemological tradition of Gaston Bachelard, Georges Canguilhem, Pierre Bourdieu and Michel Foucault, and their late reception by Rainer Diaz-Bone, this article elucidates the methodological position of constrained constructivism. Constrained constructivism is seen to embrace four main features altogether: recognition of the ever present limits of cognition; attainment of an epistemological break from everyday knowledge; use of holistic methodology; and sustainment of second-order reflexivity. The concluding part of the article discusses the methodological consequences of constrained constructivism for discourse analysis. Amongst other things, decisions about the material analyzed, compilation of the text material, research strategies, and also the interpretations of the material should be justified and motivated with regard to the epistemological limits of research. Moreover, research results should be presented in such a transparent manner that they can be intersubjectively grasped, criticized and, ideally, also revised.##

MAURER, ANDREA (Ed.)
Wirtschaftssoziologie nach Max Weber
Wiesbaden: VS Verlag 2010
283 pp., Euro 34,95; ISBN 3-531-16770-1
Keywords: Weber, M., economic sociology, capitalism, consumerism, sociology of religion, rationalization, religion and economy

Economic sociology after Max Weber

In this volume the authors want to show how a theoretically grounded and empirically fertile sociology of economy might look like; they deal with methodological principles and central notions of Weber.

SWEDBERG, RICHARD: Die Bedeutung der Weber'schen Kategorien für die Wirtschaftsoziologie [The importance of Weber's categories for economic sociology]

NORKUS, ZENONAS: Soziologische Erklärungen wirtschaftlicher Sachverhalte mit Weber [Sociological explanations of economic facts with Weber]

ERLEI, MATHIAS: Neoklassik, Institutionenökonomik und Max Weber [Neoclassic, economics of institutions, and Max Weber]

MIKL-HORKE, GERTRAUDE: Der Markt bei Weber und in der neuen Wirtschaftsoziologie [The market in Weber and in the new economic sociology]

MAURER, ANDREA: Der privat-kapitalistische Wirtschaftsbetrieb: ein wirtschaftssoziologischer Blick auf Unternehmen? [The private-capitalistic economic company. An economic-sociological perspective on companies]

RÖSSEL, JÖRG: Kapitalismus und Konsum. Determinanten und Relevanz des Konsumverhaltens in Max Webers Wirtschaftssoziologie [Capitalism and consumerism. Determinants and relevance of consumerist behavior in Max Weber's sociology of economy]

KOCH, ANNE: Die Religionssoziologie Max Webers im Lichte der neueren Kulturwissenschaft und der Religionsökonomie [The sociology of religion of Max Weber in the light of recent cultural science and economy of religion]

SCHWINN, THOMAS: Wirtschaftssoziologie als Gesellschaftstheorie? Kritische Anfragen aus einer Weber'schen Perspektive [Sociology of economy as theory of society? Critical questions from a Weberian perspective]

SCHIMANK, UWE: Max Webers Rationalisierungsthese – differenzierungstheoretisch und wirtschaftssoziologisch gelesen [Max Weber's theory of rationalization – read in a differentiation- and economic-sociological way]

SCHULZ-SCHAEFFER, INGO: Eigengesetzlichkeit, Spannungsverhältnis, Wahlverwandtschaft und Kausalität. Zum Verhältnis von Religion und Wirtschaft bei Max Weber [Autonomous law, stress relation, elective affinity and causality. On the relation of religion and economy in Max Weber]

McROBBIE, ANGELA
Top Girls. Feminismus und der Aufstieg des neoliberalen Geschlech-
terregimes. Herausgegeben von Sabine Hark und Paula-Irene Villa
Wiesbaden: VS Verlag 2010
227 pp., Euro 24.95; ISBN 3-531-16272-0
Keywords: feminism, neoliberal gender roles, gender regimes, female freedom, post-feminism

Top girls. Feminism and the rise of the neoliberal gender regime. Ed. By
Sabine Hark and Paula-Irene Villa
In this translation into German of the book the author critically assesses the
‚end of feminism' in the face of re-traditionalizations of gender regimes
which seem to become dominant. She analyzes how consumer and popular
cultures appropriate rhetoric and images of female freedom and autonomy
through which they seem to support female success. The author shows,
however, that women are in fact driven into new, post-feminist and
‚neurotic' dependencies. Thus she reflects on fashion photography, TV
series, the ‚treatment' of the body in bulimia and anorexia, body hysteria
etc.

MEUSER, MICHAEL
Geschlecht, Macht, Männlichkeit – Strukturwandel von Erwerbsarbeit und
hegemoniale Männlichkeit
Erwägen Wissen Ethik 21.2010:325-336
Keywords: masculinity, labor and masculinity, modernity and masculinity, gainful employment, employment and masculinity, subordinated masculinities, hegemonic masculinities

Gender, power, masculinity – structural change of labor and hegemonic
masculinity
##Analyzing masculinity in social sciences is ranging between theorizing
masculinity in terms of power and dominance on the one side and a
diagnosis of the present position of men in society focussing on a loss of
power on the other side. After a historical reference to the long tradition of
crisis discourses in broaching the issue of masculinity in modernity, the
article discusses the conceptual grounds of the leading category in
masculinity studies in social sciences and humanities, hegemonic
masculinity, and asks in what way the present structural transformation of
gainful employment does jeopardize hegemonic masculinity. This question

is motivated by the insight of gender studies concerning gainful employment being a central institutional pillar of hegemonic masculinity. The article ends with some open questions concerning the relation of hegemonic and subordinated masculinities.##

MOHR, HANS
Evolutionäre Ethik
Erwägen Wissen Ethik 21.2010:231-242
Keywords: evolutionary ethics, ethics and biology, memes (cultural), cultural memes, moral behavior, determinism, genetic determinism, morals and laws, laws and morals, ‚normative ethics'

Evolutionary ethics
##Evolutionary ethics aim at an understanding and judging of man's moral behaviour in view of his evolutionary disposition. This approach implies that at least parts of moral attitudes are accessible to an explanation in scientific terms. Moreover it is assumed that human moral behaviour is determined by an interaction of genetic information and cultural memes. This means that the principal patterns of our moral behaviour, the moral universals, are determined by our genetic outfit. Only the fine structure of our moral attitude is formed in the dialogue between the genetic software and the cultural meme. Along these lines we will analyze the concept of 'mixed strategies', exemplified among others by the political strategy of ‚social market-economy', and the transition from morals to law in man's cultural history. Emphasis is further laid on genetic/memetic aspects of evolutionary-economy, including the question to what extent the relationship between morals, consciousness (including free will) and responsibility may be considered a topic of evolutionary theory. In the final chapter we will consider ‚evolutionary vs. normative ethics' in view of a rational memetic evolution, as an indispensable postulate in our endangered world.##

MÜLLER, MARION & DARIUS ZIFONUN (Eds.)
Ethnowissen. Soziologische Beiträge zu ethnischer Differenzierung und Migration
Wiesbaden: VS Verlag 2010
468 pp., Euro 39.95; ISBN 3-531-16226-3

Keywords: ‚race', ethnicity, Du Bois, W.E.B., ethnomethodology, ethnic inequality, migrants, soccer, cyber-ethnicity

Ethno-knowledge. Sociological contributions to ethnic distinction and migration

BÖS, MATHIAS: ‚Rasse' und ‚Ethnizität': W.E.B. Du Bois und die wissenschaftliche Konstruktion sozialer Großgruppen in der Geschichte der US-amerikanischen Soziologie [‚Race' and ‚ethnicity': W.E.B. DuBois and the scientific construction of social macro groups in the history of US American sociology]

CORNELL, STEPHEN & DOUGLAS HARTMANN: Ethnizität und Rasse: ein konstruktivistischer Ansatz [Ethnicity and race: a constructionist approach]

WIMMER, ANDREAS: Ethnische Grenzziehungen: eine prozessorientierte Mehrebenentheorie [Ethnic delimitation: A process-oriented theory of several levels]

BERGMANN, JÖRG: Die kategoriale Herstellung von Ethnizität – Ethnomethodologische Überlegungen zur Ethnizitätsforschung [The categorial generation of ethnicity. Ethnomethodological reflections on ethnicity research]

LANGHOF, ANTONIA: ‚Ethnische Differenz' und ‚ökonomischer Verteilungskonflikt' als Schemata der Beobachtung gesellschaftlicher Konflikte [‚Ethnic difference' and ‚economic conflict of distribution' as schemes for observing societal conflict]

WATERS, MARY C.: Ethnizität als Option: nur für Weiße? [Ethnicity as an option: Only for whites?]

NECKEL, SIGHARD & FERDINAND SUTTERLÜTY: Negative Klassifikationen und ethnische Ungleichheit [Negative classifications and ethnic inequality]

SCHERSCHEL, KARIN: Dimensionen der Ungleichheit im national-staatlich stratifizierten sozialen Raum [Dimensions of inequality in the nation-state stratified social space]

LAMONT, MICHELE & SADA AKSARTOVA: Der alltägliche Kosmopolitismus einfacher Leute. Strategien zur Überwindung von Rassengrenzen zwischen Männern der Arbeiterklasse [The everyday cosmopolitism of simple people. Strategies for overcoming racial limits between men of the working class]

BRUBAKER, ROGERS: Die Diaspora des Diaspora-Konzepts [The Diaspora of the Diaspora concept]

ZIFONUN, DARIUS: Ein ‚gallisches Dorf'? Integration, Stadtteilbindung und Prestigeordnung in einem ‚Armenviertel' [A ‚Gallic village'?

Integration, neighborhood rootedness and prestige order in a ‚poor neighborhood']
SCHRÖER, NORBERT: Der ausgrenzende Vernehmer – Ein Sonderwissensbestand türkische Migranten [The excluding interviewer. A special knowledge-area of Turkish migrants]
KISSAU, KATHRIN: ‚Ethnische Sphären' im Internet [‚Ethnic spheres' in the Internet]
ESSER, HARTMUT: Ethnische Ungleichheit, ethnische Differenzierung und moderne Gesellschaft [Ethnic inequality, ethnic differentiation and modern society]
MÜLLER, MARION: Ethnische und funktionale Differenzierung: Zur Relevanz ethnisch-nationaler Zuschreibungen im Profifußball [Ethnic and functional distinction: On the relevance of ethnic-national prescriptions in professional soccer]
PLÜMECKE, TINO: Die neuen Differenzen der Lebenswissenschaften. ‚Rasse', Genetik und die ungenutzten Potentiale der Soziologie [The new differences in the life sciences. ‚Race', genetics and the unused potentials of sociology]
ZWENGEL, ALMUT: Von kulturellen Differenzen zur Kultur der Differenz. Überlegungen zu einem Paradigmenwechsel [From cultural differences to the culture of difference. Reflections on a new paradigm change]

MÜNCH, RICHARD
Der Monopolmechanismus in der Wissenschaft. Auf den Schultern von Robert K. Merton

Berliner Journal für Soziologie 20.2010:341-370
Keywords: New Public Management, ‚high impact journal', hierarchy of journals, market power, circular accumulation, competition, recognition, entrepreneurial universities, Matthew effect

##*The monopoly mechanism in science. On the shoulders of Robert K. Merton*
Quality assurance has become the guiding principle of governing research in the wake of the global diffusion of New Public Management. In this respect, the ‚high impact Journal' occupies a central place. It is shown that the production of a hierarchy of disciplinary journals furthers the monopoly mechanism in science through processes of the material production of market power and symbolically constructed exclusivity. These processes

and the rule of the Shanghai ranking enable an exclusive class of globally dominant universities to ensure the circular accumulation of economic and symbolic capital. The competition among researchers for recognition by the scientific community in terms of their contributions to the advancement of knowledge is being displaced by the competition among entrepreneurial universities for researchers, students and funds as profit generating resources. The resulting tendencies of halting the evolution of knowledge can be counteracted by measures which further the plurality of authorities for quality assurance, the building of opposing power to existing power in a system of checks and balances and by providing space for methodological anarchy.##

MÜNZEL, MARK
The end
Paideuma 56.2010:221-240
Keywords: end of anthropology, anthropology as literature, representation

##This paper was delivered as one of the 2008 Jensen Memorial Lectures, the title of which contained a printing error: a question mark following ‚the end'. It is the metaphor of the end which endows anthropology with a particular literary quality that other disciplines have lost in all their optimism. The discipline's proximity to the genre of *belles lettres* has allowed it repeatedly to revitalise this heuristically very fruitful figure of speech. Most of the contributions to this collection have not sought to declare anthropology dead, but on the contrary, to stress it's merits and argue for its continued importance, even necessity. I would like to do the same. However, I do not wish to bury talk of the end. Instead, I would rather like to stress its value as a future-oriented part of the great tradition of anthropology as literature.##

NAGEL, ALEXANDER-KENNETH
Vom Paradigma zum Pragma. Religion und Migration in relationaler Perspektive
Sociologia Internationalis 48.2010:221-246
Keywords: paradigm, pragma, relational sociology, religion and sociology, migration

From paradigm to pragma. Religion and migration in relational perspective
##In recent years the American discussion about "relational sociology" has finally reached the German sociological debate and came to be promoted with a particular paradigmatic furor. For the time being, however, the programmatic claims in this debate have been at odds with the realities of applied research. In this article I will explore the chances and challenges of a relational perspective with regard to questions of religion and migration. I will argue that the heuristic value of a relational approach is to complement a widespread image of religious migrant communities as isolated entities and hermetic cultural enclaves with a more optimistic notion of embedded and embedding social spaces. Instead of reinventing the sociological wheel I suggest a relational reading of existing concepts of diaspora. Following these conceptual considerations I will outline a number of research areas and questions which result from a relational perspective on religion and migration.##

NEVELING, PATRICK
Einleitende Überlegungen: Wissen um Veränderung – Entwicklung, Geschichte, sozialer Wandel
Sociologus 60.2010:1-14
Keywords: change, transformation social transformation, theory formation

##*Introductory Remarks - The Production of Knowledge about Change: Development, History, Social Transformation*
The following paper briefly introduces the three contributions to this issue on "Notions of Change". Furthermore, some of the basic concepts with which this issue is concerned are discussed. These are the question of how to demarcate historical eras, the question of the range of theories in the social sciences and the question of the problematic entanglement of theories in the social sciences with hegemonic discourses that proclaim a distinctive newness of the respective present.##

ORANSKAIA, TATIANA & BARBARA SCHULER (Eds.)
Göttinnen, Heldinnen und Herrscherinnen in Asien und Afrika
Frankfurt/M.: Lang Verlag 2010
203 pp., Euro 39.80; ISBN 3-631-59218-2

Keywords: goddesses, heroines, female rulers, myths, political myths, memory, Lori Mata

Goddesses, heroines, and female rulers in Asia and Africa
POHL, MANFRED: Hōjō Masako: Eine Frau gegen Japans Kaiser [Hōjō Masako. A woman contra the Japanese emperor]
STUMPFELDT, HANS: Scheusal und Buddha der Zukunft: die Kaiserin Wu Tse-t'ien (684-704) [Monster and Buddha of the future. The empress Wu Tse-t'ien (684-704)]
SCHULZ-ZINDA, YVONNE: Die Revolutionärin Qiu Jin (1875-1907): der Stoff, aus dem die Heldin ist [The revolutionary Qiu Jin (1875-1907): A substance out of which the heroine is made]
ENGELBERT, THOMAS: Göttinnen und Heldinnen in Vietnam: Dorfgemeinde und dörfliche Kultstätten der Việt [Goddesses and heroines in Vietnam: The village community and village cult places of the Việt]
HEINSCHKE, MARTINA: Politische Mythen und Geschlechterordnung im vormodernen Java [Political myths and gender order in premodern Java]
SCHULER, BARBARA: Was wird erinnert? – Gewalt und Ruhm als Erinnerungssignaturen [What is being remembered? Violence and glory signatures of recollection]
ORANSKAIA, TATIANA: Lori Mata: Eine Göttin aus der Kaste der Straßenakrobaten [Lori Mata: A goddess of the caste of street acrobats]
WÖBKE, RITA: Aspekte weiblicher Existenz in Afrika [Aspects of female existence in Africa]

ÖSTERLUND-PÖTZSCH, SUSANNE
Pedestrian Art. The Tourist Gait as Tactic and Performance
Ethnologia Europaea 40,2.2010:14-28
Keywords: walking practices, performance, everyday life, tourism, flânerie, practice

##Our walking as tourists is in many respects different from our "non-tourist" or everyday walking. Building on John Urry's well-known concept of the "tourist gaze", I suggest the coinage of the "tourist gait" for describing a type of walking characterized, among other things, by a heightened awareness of sensory impressions and an active involvement with one's surroundings. In this article, I explore how the tourist gait can be employed as a tactic for claiming and experiencing space in our home environs. By comparing tourist gait practices with the phenomenon of flânerie, the performance element contained in everyday pedestrianism emerges. Quotidian walking can demonstrate great creativity and is definitively much more tharr just a means of transportation.##

OVERDICK, THOMAS
Photographing culture. Anschauung und Anschaulichkeit in der Ethnographie
(Kulturwissenschaftliche Technikforschung 2)
Zürich: Chronos Verlag 2010
338 pp., Euro 32,50; ISBN 3-0340-1044-3
Keywords: visual anthropology, photography

Photographing culture. Viewing in ethnography
The author integrates photography in the range of methods in fieldwork in the cultural sciences. However, present ethnographic practice in Folklore Studies seems to be sceptical regarding photography, even though there is a boom of discussing photography since the 1990s, but a „photographic discourse in the sense of visual ethnography" has not been taking place so far. The author prsents an epistemologically and media-founded study based on Anglo-American *visual anthropology* – stressing the epistemological potential of photographic practice.

PRAGER, CHRISTIAN M.
Die kognitionswissenschaftliche Erforschung von Religion
Zeitschrift für Ethnologie 135.2010:219-232
Keywords: cognitive sciences, religion and cognitivism, culture and cognitive science

##Cognitive science research of religion
The purpose of this review paper is to discuss the relevance of cognitive science to the field of cultural anthropology with special emphasis on religious studies. Cognition as the mental capacity to represent and process information is a striking part of the mental apparatus. It is concerned with the manner in which people represent and interpret their natural, social and cultural environment. According to the standard model in the social sciences only socio-cultural factors could explain cultural and religious phenomena - its natural foundations, however, have been largely ignored so far and mark the focus of the cognitive science of cultural studies. According to this view culture can also be regarded as constellations of

mental and public representations communicated and regulated by human minds. Thus, a cognitive science of culture and religion differs from the social science standard model by insisting that both domains are to be understood by-products of ordinary cognitive processes and a cognitive science of culture and religion seeks to explain the natural foundations of culture that also includes religious phenomena.##

REICHERTZ, JO
Die Macht der Worte und der Medien. 3. Auflage
Wiesbaden: VS Verlag 2010
333 pp., Euro 29.95; ISBN 3-531-17242-2
Keywords: media utilization, performativity, TV as actor, actors, internet, trust and internet, texts and interpretation, representation and texts, communication theory

The power of words and the media. 3rd edition
This collection of articles/essays focusing on the media inquires into their force and power, which is one of the central questions of present-day society. So, questions are under which conditions TV will have effects (on the people), how media communication can be used in professional work, in companies, by consultants, by scholars. TV is discussed as an actor, institutionalization as a precondition of performativity, effects of movies on personal action, questions of the internet in connection with trust, advertisement, sports as a communicative integration ritual, the interpretation of homepages, and finally, what words can do and cannot do.

RITSCHEL, GREGOR
Backpackers: Betwixt and between
Cargo. Zeitschrift für Ethnologie 30.2010:7-16
Keywords: backpacking, ethnography of backpacking, liminality, tourism

Ritschel reflects on his travels and experiences as a backpacker (in South America), using liminality (van Gennep and Turner), Bourdieu and a paper of Anders Sørensen to frame his thoughts.

RÖSCHENTHALER, UTE
Tauschsphären. Geschichte und Bedeutung eines wirtschaftsethnologischen Konzepts
Anthropos 105.2010:157-177
Keywords: exchange, Bohannan, P., Tiv, economic anthropology, prestige and goods

Spheres of exchange. History and importance of a concept in economic anthropology
##This article examines the concept of the spheres of exchange or transaction spheres in economic anthropology. It starts with the most well-known example, the three hierarchically ordered and morally connotated spheres of exchange which Paul Bohannan found among the Tiv in Eastern Nigeria. It discusses the criticisms which Bohannan's work has provoked and traces the concept's history to two main schools of thought. The comprehension of the spheres of exchange in their broader context of economy and society makes clear that they are not an exotic phenomenon, vanishing under the influence of Western culture, but a structuring strategy generally found in societies, and with which certain social groups justify claims to prestigious goods and services.##

ROTHE, ANNELIE
Das große Bild vor Augen: Wie die Kognitionsethnologie zurück zu den Kognitionswissenschaften finden kann
Zeitschrift für Ethnologie 135.2010:259-274
Keywords: cognitive sciences, psychology and cognitivism, decline of cognitivism, cognitive anthropology, cross-cultural psychology

##*Don't lose the big picture! How to get cognitive anthropology back into the cognitive sciences*
The tangible presence of cognitive anthropology decreased strongly within the cognitive sciences and even within socio-cultural anthropology during the last approximately three decades. Reasons for this development can be found in four different factors which are outlined in this paper and used as impetus for change. From the perspective of young academics or students of anthropology, possibilities and ideas are discussed that might help improving the rather poor condition cognitive anthropology is in and encourage or challenge senior scientists to become aware of their responsibilities. As one topic for interdisciplinary exchange between cognitive anthropology and other cognitive sciences, studies on the

influence of cultural self-construal on cognition are introduced. These are usually conducted within cross-cultural psychology, but provide an intersection between psychology and anthropology as well as an opportunity for fruitful interdisciplinary collaboration in teaching and research. At the end of this paper, remarks on rather practical than theoretical contemplations summarize miscellaneous preconditions and opportunities for (re-)establishing a strong anthropological share in the big picture of cognition.##

SCHEVE, CHRISTIAN VON
Die emotionale Struktur sozialer Interaktion: Emotionsexpression und soziale Ordnungsbildung
Zeitschrift für Soziologie 39.2010:346-362
Keywords: emotional structure, interaction, order and emotion, expression and emotion, facial expression, decoding expression

##*The Emotional Structure of Social Interaction: The Expression of Emotion and the Emergence of Social Order*
This contribution investigates functions of emotion in social interaction and their role in the emergence and reproduction of social structures and social order. It assumes that the elicitation of emotion is fundamentally dependent on the social environment and that emotions go hand in hand with characteristic action tendencies. On this basis, it is argued that the facial expression of emotion is particularly implicated in generating patterns of social action and interaction. First, it is shown that the encoding of facial expression combines hard-wired physiological principles on the one hand and socially learned aspects on the other, leading to more fine-grained and socially differentiated "dialects" of emotional expression. Second, it is argued that the decoding of facial expression is contingent upon this combination, so that reciprocal attributions of emotional states, situational interpretations, and action tendencies are more effective within rather than across social units. Third, this conjunction affects the conditions for emotional contagion, which is shown to be more effective within social units exhibiting similar encoding and decoding characteiistics and thus aligns emotions and action tendencies in a coherent, yet socially differentiated fashion. Taken together, these interactional processes show that emotions facilitate the structuring of social interaction and the emergence of social order##

SCHMIDT, VOLKER H.
Die ostasiatische Moderne - eine Moderne „eigener" Art?
Berliner Journal für Soziologie 20.2010:123-152
Keywords: modernities, multiple modernities, western modernity, Eisenstadt, S.

##*East Asian modernity – A "distinct" modernity?*
The article casts doubt on the claim of Eisenstadt and other culturalists that East Asia constitutes a distinct modernity, one that differs fundamentally from Western modernity. Following a brief reconstruction of key modernization theoretical premises against which this claim is directed, it compares the five largest Western countries with the currently most advanced exemplars of East Asian modernity. The findings show that the two regions are remarkably similar in virtually all respects that matter from a modernization theoretical viewpoint. The article then goes on to assess the relevance of the evidence held against modernization theory by Eisenstadt and his followers. As it turns out, this evidence presents no challenge to modernization theory whatsoever. Moreover, its epistemological status is dubious given that multiple modernists lack a sufficiently worked-out theory of modernity in whose light the social theoretic significance of empirical observations could be assessed. Drawing upon the differentiation theoretical tradition, an alternative approach is outlined that addresses multiple modernists' substantive concerns without falling into the trap of essentializing diversity. However, utilizing this approach for the comparison between Western and East Asian modernity subverts the very idea of a uniform West against which the notion of a distinctly East Asian modernity is posited.##

SCHNEIDERS, THORSTEN GERALD (Ed.)
Islamfeindlichkeit. Wenn die Grenzen der Kritik verschwimmen. 2., aktualisierte und erweiterte Auflage
Wiesbaden: VS Verlag 2010
498 pp., 49.95; ISBN 3-531-17440-2
Keywords: Islamophobia, Muslims, critique of Islam, history of Islamophobia

Islamophobia. When the borders of criticism get blurred. 2nd., updated and enlarged edition
The thirty papers in this book – by social scientists, historians of religions, political scientists etc. – are divided into four sections, namely: starting points of Islamophobia in German society (historical and theological

causes, processes in history, narratives, Islamophobia connected with immigration); the current situation of Islamophobia (distinct topics discussed in the media, regarding women, building of mosques, in schools, in the media...); institutionalized Islamophobia (in political parties and the Churches), and personal Islamophobia (descriptions of cases of well-known individuals). The editor sees ‚pure ressentiments' as a frequent background for Islam criticism, and there is a ‚dogmatic attitude of defence' among Muslims, which does not consider any critique. The contributions in this book analyze many aspects of this overall phenomenon.

SCHOLZ, ALEXANDER
Entwicklungszusammenarbeit und normative Ordnungen. Eine ethno-phänomenologische Problemskizze in entwicklungsethnologischer Absicht
Cargo. Zeitschrift für Ethnologie 30.2010:59-68
Keywords: development, normative orders, norms, values and development aid, intersubjectivity

Development cooperation and normative orders
Inspired by a research project on „normative orders" and a relation with „development cooperation" by an un-named university Scholz discusses: 1. Lifeworlds and their connection with orders claiming universal validity, and development activity. He then generates an „ethno-phenomenological perspective" on these research questions by introducing three types of intersubjectivity, and by qualifying two object settings and their orders. Finally, results of this operation are applied to the introductory question.

SCHULZ-SCHAEFFER, INGO
Praxis, handlungstheoretisch betrachtet
Zeitschrift für Soziologie 39.2010:319-336
Keywords: practice, theory of action, action theory, embodied practice, tacit knowledge

Practice. A Theory-of-Action Perspective
Theorists of the "practice turn" argue that the concept of action should be replaced by the concept of embodied social practices because they assume that the tacit knowledge and skills of social practices are much more fundamental for understanding human social conduct than the action

theorists' supposedly individual and rational actions. The aim of the paper is to show that the role of tacit knowledge and skills can be analyzed more clearly and in a more refined way within a theory-of-action framework, especially by drawing on recent approaches which add to the concept of action further considerations concerning the definition of the situation##

STICHWEH, RUDOLF
Der Fremde. Studien zu Soziologie und Sozialgeschichte
(Suhrkamp Taschenbuch Wissenschaft 1924)
Berlin: Suhrkamp Verlag 2010
213 pp., Euro 10,-; ISBN 3-518-29524-3
Keywords: strangers, foreigners, alterity

The stranger. Studies in sociology and social history
A dozen articles, previously published, deal with ‚the stranger' from a largely sociological (and hardly anthropological) perspective, by including inspiration from various other disciplines (philosophy, history, political science) and the history of ideas in a general sense; i.e., in the widest possible perspective. Thus, the author discusses how humans find and delimit themselves, the role of strangeness in academia, in the self-description of Europe in historical times, especially Early Modernity, and then the break in modernity, where all others are strangers, or nobody is. It is argued that self-analysis in modernity ‚invents forms of minimal sympathy and universal indifference which determine our relations with all others'.

THELEN, TATJANA
Modernität, Mangelwirtschaft und Postsozialismus. Probleme ethnologischer und soziologischer Theoriebildung angesichts gesellschaftlicher Veränderung
Sociologus 60.2010:15-40
Keywords: theory production, anthropological theory, modernization theory, postsocialism

##*Modernity, the economy of shortage and postsocialism: Problems of anthropological and sociological theory-building in the face of social change*

The central question posed in this article is, why despite of almost ideal conditions no genuine theory building of social change took place. Instead, a neo-institutional interpretation dominated Anthropology, and Sociology saw the revival of modernisation theory. The article traces these characteristic lines of argumentation and shows that both strands necessarily led to analyses of both socialist and postsocialist societies as in deficit. The following reflections on studies concerned with work and gender relations show that only if normative assumptions, especially concerning the distinction between public and private sphere, are abandoned the prospect for new theoretical reflections emerge.##

WALDENFELS, BERNHARD
Sinne und Künste im Wechselspiel. Modi ästhetischer Erfahrung
(Suhrkamp Taschenbuch Wissenschaft 1973)
Berlin: Suhrkamp Verlag 2010
409 pp., Euro 14,-; ISBN 3-518-29573-1
Keywords: aesthetic experience, arts, senses and arts, otherness and senses, theater, Merleau-Ponty, M., healing, pain, perception

The interplay of senses and the arts. Modi of aesthetic experience
In this systematic philosophical assessment of sensual experience Waldenfels discusses the perception, effects, power, utilization, traces etc. of pictures, images, of sound, movement (dance, theater), theater as the location of otherness (alterity), food and feelings, and finally pain and healing as feedback to sensual experiences. In doing so, he draws on Nietzsche, phenomenology, Merleau-Ponty, Heidegger and many others as well as on classical (western) philosophy. Recurrent is the topic of culture, and otherness in such experiences.

WALTERMANN, SARAH
Reif für die Insel? Die Insel als Ort des zweiten Anfangs
Cargo. Zeitschrift für Ethnologie 30.2010:17-20
Keywords: islands, fantasy

The island as a location of a second beginning
Waltermann reflects on islands as objects of fantasy and briefly discusses literary works and movies of this kind (Daniel Defoe and others), and she

discusses the island as a „second beginning" in the sense of Deleuze – and finally there are anthropologists as „lone wolves" pursuing their objects of research.

WERRON, TOBIAS
Direkte Konflikte, indirekte Konkurrenzen. Unterscheidung und Vergleich zweier Formen des Kampfes
Zeitschrift für Soziologie 39.2010:302-318
Keywords: conflict, indirect competition, struggle, competition

##*Direct conflict, Indirect Competition Differentiation and Comparison of two Forms of Struggle*
This article develops and applies a sociological differentiation between conflict and competition in three distinct steps: (1) Conflicts can be understood as dynamic processes of communication which are initiated by a concatenation of contradictions of contradictions; they are a direct form of struggle that depends on mutual communication between the parties. (2) In contrast, following Georg Simmel, in situations of competition parties become rivals only once they try to win the favor of a third party; competition is therefore an indirect form of struggle that depends on observation by third parties but does not require contact between the opponents. (3) This differentiation opens up new possibilities of comparison, and it is used here to analyze exemplary cases of coexistence and collision between the two forms. The heuristic advantage of the differentiation is particularly salient in cases in which the public becomes involved as a third party which brings about the special dynamics of modern competition as a "fight of all for all" (Simmel). It is in these cases that the differentiation of the fwo forms of struggle gains particular theoretical significance and practical importance##

WILK, NICOLE M. (Ed.)
Esswelten. Über den Funktionswandel der täglichen Kost
(Welt – Körper – Sprache 8)
Frankfurt/M.: Lang Verlag 2010
198 pp., Euro 47.80; ISBN 3-631-58670-9
Keywords: food and culture, food habits, cooking and culture, semiology, McDonaldization, literature and food

Worlds of eating. On changing functions of everyday diet
The articles in this volume are based on a workshop at the conference of the „Deutsche Gesellschaft für Semiotik", Stuttgart 2008, approaching the topic from „negative" perspectives such as the image of the fat human being, disgust, bulimia, shame, etc.

KLOTTER, CHRISTOPH: Die Trägheit der Zeichen – neue Aspekte einer Semiologie des Essens [The sluggishness of sign.s New aspects of a semiology of eating]

LEMKE, HARALD: Anderes – Selbst – Verkörpern – Bausteine einer gastrosophischen Anthropologie und Subjekttheorie [Alterity, self, embodiment. Stepping stones of a gastrosophic anthropology and theory of the subject]

MALITS, ANDREA: Kulinarik als subversive Kunstform – Kochkunst und Ekel in der „Cena Trimalchionis" [Culinaric as a subversive form of art. Cooking and disgust in the „Cena Trimalchionis"]

BAYER, FRAUKE: ‚Der Rest ist Essen'. Der alimentäre Code des orgiastischen Essakts in Georg Brittings Roman „Lebenslauf eines dicken Mannes, der Hamlet hieß" [The rest is eating. The alimentary code of the orgiastic act of eating in Georg Britting's novel „Lebenslauf eines dicken Mannes, der Hamlet hieß"]

VARWIG, OLIVIA: Das Schlaraffenland im (Anti-)Entwicklungsroman – Zur Literarisierung des Essens in Goethes „Wilhelm Meisters Lehrjahre" und Thomas Manns „Bekenntnisse des Hochstaplers Felix Krull" [The Cockaigne in the (anti-)character-development novel. On the literalization of eating in Goethe's „Wilhelm Meisters Lehrjahre" and Thomas Mann's „Bekenntnisse des Hochstaplers Felix Krull"]

HÄCKER, ANDREAS: Politik und Sinnlichkeit des Fastens – George Taboris „Hungerkünstler" und weitere Produktionen des Bremer Theaterlabors [Politics and the sensuality of fasting. George Tabori's „Hungerkünstler" and other productions of the Bremen theater laboratory]

SEIDLER, MIRIAM: Alles Peanuts!? Semiotik der Speise in Martin Walsers Roman „Der Lebenslauf der Liebe" [Just peanuts? Semiotics of food in Martin Walser's novel „Der Lebenslauf der Liebe"]

BOEHME, TIM CASPAR: Nutrimentalpathologien des Alltags [Nutrimental pathologies of everyday life]

BARTSCH, SILKE: Jugendesskultur – Von der Tischgemeinschaft zum „Dauersnacken"? [Youth food culture. From commensality to „permanent snacking"]

WILK, NICOLE M.: „Wissen, wo's herkommt." McDonaldisiertes Weltwissen [„Knowing where it comes from". McDonaldized world knowledge]

WINDMÜLLER, SONJA
Rhythm – a world language? Reflections on movement-oriented cultural analysis
Ethnologia Europaea 40,1.2010:30-41
Keywords: Rhythm, movement and cultural analysis, cultural analysis, music and rhythm

##The article explores the idea and practice of rhythm as a subject as well as a perspective of cultural analysis that points to the physical dimension of culture, the social effects of bodily movements. Against holistic (and essentialist) conceptualisations of rhythm, the paper argues for a more detailed, multi-perspective approach, facing concrete phenomena in their specific and larger contexts, their functions and content and not least their interrelations and cross-references. The focus here is on a popular as well as questionable theoretical and practical model in a key area of rhythmic expressions: the model of rhythm as a (musical) „world language". It can be shown how different, even (supposedly) competing concepts of rhythm are affiliated, how explicit and subliminal models and practices are adjoined by further meaning, and, finally, how they develop culture-constituting qualities.##

WOLFSTELLER, RENE
Die Grenzen der „Identität". Vorschläge für einen interdisziplinären Forschungsansatz
Cargo. Zeitschrift für Ethnologie 30.2010:31-39
Keywords: identity, discourse on identity, ethnography

The limits of „identity". Proposal for an interdisciplinary approach
With Brubaker, Eickelpasch, Hacking, Latour, Straub and others the author discusses the present state of „identity" – what the concept can do and what not. And he concludes by deemphasizing theoretical abstractions (of various disciplines) and instead promotes ethnographic anthropological work in concrete cases, as recommended by Geertz.

ZEITSCHRIFT FÜR KULTURAUSTAUSCH
Stuttgart: Institut für Auslandsbeziehungen 60.2010
Keywords: Great Britain, body, e-volution, digital change, German-ness

The individual issues deal with the following topics:
60,1.2010: Großbritannien [Great Britain]
60,2.2010: Körper [Body]
60,3.2010: E-volution. Wie uns die digitale Welt verändert [E-volution. How the digital world changes us]
60,4.2010: Das Deutsche in der Welt [The German in the world]

ZIAI, ARAM
From Development Discourse to the Discourse of Globalisation - Changing Forms of Knowledge about change in North-South Relations and their Political Repercussions
Sociologus 60.2010:41-70
Keywords: globalization, development, north-south relations, knowledge, forms of knowledge

##The article argues that in the field of North-South relations, predominant conceptions of social change have been transformed during the last decades. The discourse of ‚development' which used to be dominant, has been gradually replaced by a discourse of 'globalisation'. The article engages in a comparative analysis of the turo discouises, their underlying principles and the political practices rendered possible by them.##

ZUCKERHUT, PATRICIA
Von der Gewaltdebatte in Anthropologie und Sozialwissenschaften hin zu einer feministischen Analyse geschlechtlich konnotierter Gewalt
Zeitschrift für Ethnologie 135.2010:275-304
Keywords: gender and violence, violence, sexualized violence, feminism, legitimacy, intersectionality

##*From the discussion on violence in anthropology and social sciences to a feminist analysis of gendered violence*
The article starts with a brief summary of some of the debates on gendered violence in social sciences, focusing on the definition of the concept, its

significance in human society and its social meanings. This is supplemented by considerations in the field of social and cultural anthropology about the question of legitimacy as a criterion of violence. The importance of dealing with questions like, who is legitimated to exercise violence and in what context, will be stressed. Besides this also the funcion of violence is shown as to be an important aspect of analysis. The central findings of these discussions will be looked at with regard to their relevance for a feminist (intersecional) exploration of gendered violence. In the end five points will be extracted as starting point of analysis.##

AFRICA

ALBER, ERDMUTE ET AL. (Eds.)
Verwandtschaft heute. Positionen, Ergebnisse und Perspektiven
Berlin: Reimer Verlag 2010
335 pp., Euro 29.90; ISBN 3-496-02832-1
Keywords: kinship, exchange, genealogy, Wodaabe, transcultural kinship, reciprocity

Kinship today. Positions, results, and perspectives
TIMM, ELISABETH: „Ich fühle mich absolut verwandt": Entgrenzung, Personalisierung und Gouvernementalität von Verwandtschaft am Beispiel der populären Genealogie [„I feel absolutely related". Delimitation, personalization and governmentality of kinship in the case of popular genealogy]
BOVENSIEPEN, JUDITH: „Ich gebe dir mein Kind". Pflegschafts- und Tauschbeziehungen in Osttimor [„I give you my child" Guardianship and exchange relations in eastern Timor]
SCHAREIKA, NIKOLAUS: Rituell gezeugt: Verwandtschaft als symbolische Interaktion bei den Wodaabe Südostnigers [Ritually generated: kinship as symbolical interaction among the Wodaabe of Southeast Niger]
ALEX, GABRIELE: Tamilische Verwandtschaft im Wandel [Changing Tamilian kinship]
BEER, BETTINA: Interethnische Beziehungen und transkulturelle Verwandtschaft an einem Beispiel aus Papua-Neuguinea [Interethnic relations and transcultural kinship in a case of Papua New Guinea]
DROTBOHM, HEIKE: Begrenzte Verbindlichkeiten: Zur Bedeutung von Reziprozität und Kontribution in transnationalen Familien [Limited obligations: On the importance of reciprocity and contribution in transnational families]
FISCHER, GUNDULA: „Verwandtschaft schafft Arbeit – Arbeit schafft Verwandtschaft": Überlegungen zur Konstruktion von Verwandtschaft in einem tansanischen Betrieb [Kinship creates work – work creates kinship. Reflections on the construction of kinship in a Tanzanian company]
THELEN, TATJANA: Kinning im Alter: Verbundenheit und Sorgebeziehungen ostdeutscher Senior/Innen [Kinning in old age. Company and care relations of East German senior citizens]

HAUSER-SCHÄUBLIN, BRIGITTA: Manipulierte Substanzen, rekonfigurierte Verwandtschaften: Humantechnologische Prozesse und ihre Bedeutung für die Verwandtschaft zwischen Normativität und Flexibilität [Manipulated substances, reconfigured kinships: Human-technological processes and their meaning for kinship between normativity and flexibility]

ALBER, ERDMUTE & TABEA HÄBERLEIN: Ethnologische Generationenforschung in Afrika [Ethnological research on generations in Africa]

SCHNEGG, MICHAEL & JULIA PAULI: Namibische Wahlverwandtschaften: zur Aktualität von Struktur und Handlungsfreiheit in der Verwandtschaftsethnologie [Namibian elective affinities: On the topicality of structure and freedom for action in kinship anthropology]

ALBER, ERDMUTE, TABEA HÄBERLEIN & JEANNETT MARTIN
Changing webs of kinship: Spotlights on West Africa
Africa Spectrum 45,3.2010:43-67
Keywords: kinship, changing kinship, marriage, parent-child relations, conflict

##Changes in kinship relations are part of the broad social change in all African societies. This article highlights trends and characteristics of changing kinship relations in West Africa. Its analysis focuses on the twentieth century, which was shaped by the colonial conquest and profound societal transformations like the political independence of the African colonies. In analysing three important kinship relations - parent-child relations, marriage, and care for the elderly - this article depicts the trends and conditions of historical change of these relationships. It also shows whether and how these changes are accompanied by conflict, and how people refer to the different ways of dealing with those conflicts. The article is based on empirical data from three thematically intertwined research projects.##

ANDRESEN, HENNING
Staatlichkeit in Afrika. Muss Entwicklungshilfe scheitern?
Frankfurt/M.: Brandes & Apsel 2010
216 pp., Euro 19.90; ISBN 3-86099-671-3
Keywords: delelopment aid, statehood, clientelism, patrimonialism, neo-patrimonialism, corruption, exploitation

Statehood in Africa. Is development aid destined to fail?
Frequently, historical and economic exploitation are named as reasons for present-day developmental failure in Africa south of the Sahara. The author asks which interrelationships exist between the African state, socioculture, and development aid. He shows how currently the state has become an instrument of power maintenance and self-enrichment, and how a weak state impedes development and successful foreign aid. On the other hand, the author opines, development aid and other foreign intervention make the African state even less capable and efficient. He describes the traditional patrimonial system of rule and the present neo-patrimonial one; the role of African ‚sociocultures' and results of 50 years of development aid. The last chapter is devoted to finding ways to go beyond this dilemma, including tackling the question of how realistic these proposals are.

ASSERATE, ASFA-WOSSEN
Eike Haberland und die Ethnologie Äthiopiens
Paideuma 56.2010:23-32
Keywords: Haberland, E.

Eike Haberland and the anthropology of Ethiopia
This paper is based on the Frobenius lecture, Frankfurt, of 2009, and describes Haberland's work and the anthropological „environment" in Frankfurt, including other anthropologists of that era.

BECK, ROSE MARIE
Urban languages in Africa
Africa Spectrum 45,3.2010:11-41
Keywords: language formation, urban languages, linguistic practices, generation of languages, modernities

##Against the backdrop of current research on the city, urbanity is understood to be a distinct way of life in which (in the spatial, factual and historical dimensions) processes of densification and heterogenization are perceived as acts of sociation. Urbanization is thus understood to include and produce structuration processes autonomously; this also includes autonomous linguistic practices, which are reflected as sediments of everyday knowledge in language and thus create the instruments needed for facilitating and generalizing such urbanization: urban languages. In this conceptual context, which looks at cities in Africa from the point of view of language sociology, two large phases of urbanization can be distinguished in Africa. The first phase is related to trade networks and cultural *métissage* of small groups of middlemen. The second phase, characterized by efforts to deal with Africa's colonial history and to catch up with "the world", presses ahead with the development of an autonomous, authentic modernity. The reconstruction of the development undergone especially by the more recent urban languages raises questions about the connotations of urbanization and modernization in contemporary Africa: on the one hand, dissociation from colonial legacies as well as from the postcolonial political elites, impotent administrations, and tribalist instrumentalizations of language and language policies; on the other, quite the reverse - the creation of autonomous African modernities that include the city (and the state), brought about by the interplay of both local dynamics and global flows.##

BECKER, GERD
Warum Aristoteles wissenschaftliche Filme gedreht hätte. Überlegungen zur Theoriefähigkeit des Bildes anhand der Erfahrungen mit dem Film ‚L'art du désert"
Zeitschrift für Ethnologie 135.2010:1-22
Keywords: films, documentary films, scholarly films, theory and film, cinematographic documentaries, phenomena as statements, non-verbal (film) statements

Why Aristotle would have made scientific films - Can images express theory? Reflections on filmwork in Morocco
##"How are ideas about the tourist-destination Morocco produced and communicated to the visitors?", we asked in a research project funded by Deutsche Forschungsgemeinschaft (DFG). Based on fieldwork and empirical studies in Morocco, our focus was on contributing to a theory of this particular form of transcultural communication. We considered applying visual research methods and presenting findings in cinematographic form essential for studies in the image-based field of tourism.
Besides texts we prepared cinematographic documentaries for publication. The film *L'Art du Désert* as discussed in this paper is Just a first step on the way exploring the scientific potenzial of visual media. Can images be used to communicate theoretical insights? To allow for discussion of this

question and to further develop methodological strategies we decided to present our preliminary results.

In non-abstract images our video-material shows processes of communicating culture in Morocco. We see how those who offer services in tourism interact with their clients. Editing the takes in particular ways allows us to unveil specific patterns of behaviour. Juxtaposing images becomes a method of analysis. Cuts introduce meaning. Statements are made with the techniques of montage. In a non-verbal way we get insight into the principles that guide the phenomena. And that is precisely our understanding of what is a theory: giving insight into the principles behind phenomena. So theory is expressed in a purely visual form.##

BEMILE, SEBASTIAN K.
Dàgàrà proverbs
(Sprache und Oralität in Afrika 25)
Berlin: Reimer Verlag 2010
342 pp., Euro 79,-; ISBN 3-496-02834-5
Keywords, Dàgàrà proverbs, proverbs of Dàgàrà

The present selection of proverbs for publication is based upon a corpus of actually attested Dàgàrà utterances. Here, I have placed emphasis on "quality", currency or popularity and personal knowledge and interest, i.e. I have selected from my collection those proverbs that I think are well formulated, popular or addressing current and historical issues which appeal to me most and which might also appeal to my readers. It should, however, be said here and now that I do not know all Dàgàrà proverbs and their variants in the different dialects. Thus, I cannot claim that I have collected all the most popular or suitable ones for the purpose of this book. Over the years, I have subjected them to constant examination and revision in order to achieve an accurate version of each proverb, to account for different varieties of the same proverb either in one and the same Dàgàrà dialect or from cross-dialect perspectives on form and content. I have also tried to avoid or to eliminate extraneous data but have exercised no deliberate censorship.## The order of the book is: a rather theoretical 15-page preface dealing with types of proverbs, questions of definition, present stage of research, selection and arrangement. It follows an introduction (chapter 1) discussing geographical aspects, historical background, cultural attitudes and ,realms' (such as religion, food, education, respect, gender...), and the 2nd chapter deals with literary and linguistic aspects. The corpus of

proverbs has translations into four, sometimes five languages (the fifth being Latin). The second part of the book groups and discusses the proverbs according to area of life (like: activity, destiny, eating, family, human nature, human relations...), i.e. in contexts.

BERGSTRESSER, HEINRICH
Nigeria. Macht und Ohnmacht am Golf von Guinea
Frankfurt/M.: Brandes & Apsel 2010
268 pp., Euro 24.90; ISBN -386099-672-0

Keywords: nationbuilding, Biafra War, resources and power, oil resources, elites and power

Nigeria. Power and powerlessness at the Gulf of Guinea
Nigeria is the biggest ,Christian-Islamic' state in the world and simultaneously the most densely populated part of Africa, and Nigerians are the biggest African overseas diaspora. The state has enormous oil and gas reserves. Since 1960 there are attempts to establish a nation – on the basis of this ethnically and religiously highly complex setting – after about a dozen military *coups d'état*. In this process, the Biafra War serves as an implict state doctrine for the elites – to avoid a comparable conflict at all costs. This setting, plus the aim to equally distribute the income accruing from oil and gas among themselves, serves as ideological ,doctrines' and framework for the elites of this state. Chapters deal with a discussion of the wealth of resources in the state, the Biafra War, the multiethnic state, new and old alliances, and new developments which complicate the situation and make it more intransparent.

BOCHOW, ASTRID
Intimität und Sexualität vor der Ehe. Gespräche über Ungesagtes in Kumasi und Endwa, Ghana
(Beiträge zur Afrika-Forschung 44)
Berlin: Lit Verlag 2010
330 pp., Euro 29.90; ISBN 3-643-10688-9

Keywords: love, marriage, pentecostal churches, urbanism, pre-marital relations, ,globalized love'

Intimacy and sexuality before marriage. Conversations on the unuttered in Kumasi und Endwa, Ghana
This book is based on field research in Assin Endwa and Kumasi (p.91). Bochow first discusses intimacy in pre-marital relations, its concepts and contexts, in Africa generally, and in Akan societies. The next part comprises the fieldwork during which she has focused on the Valentine's Day, in schools and the universities there, and Part III is devoted to discussing the time before marriage in the context of pentecostal churches: planning marriage and plans for professional achievement of young urban people. Here, Bochow focuses on marriage, change and renewal in pentecostal preaching and church practice – how young people prepare for marriage etc. The discussion deals with ‚globalized love' in pentecostal discourse, and in the end Bochow summarized her fieldwork insights regarding love, intimacy, and marriage.

DESPLAT, PATRICK
Heilige Stadt – Stadt der Heiligen. Ambivalenzen und Kontroversen islamischer Heiligkeit in Harar, Äthiopien
(Mainzer Beiträge zur Afrikaforschung 24)
Köln: Köppe Verlag 2010
293 pp., Euro 39.80; ISBN 3-89645-824-7
Keywords: Islam, sacredness in Islam, universalist Islam, local Islam, saints in Islam

Sacred city – city of saints. Ambivalences and controversies of Islamic sacredness in Harar, Ethiopia
Desplat's study, based on fieldwork, asks how sacredness in a certain place and time affects present-day society – exemplified in Harar – and how it interacts with „global flows" of Islamic reform processes. The author analyzes the dynamic relation between public discourses of religious practice and societal change. He shows how the debate on sacredness in Islam not only represents a controversy on theological issues but a competitive battle between social groups way beyond the local setting of sacredness, and the culturalization of religious practices and sacred places is a central facet of this dispute. Thus, the present study deals with a general problem of anthropologically inspired research on Islam: Is it possible to explain the heterogeneous lifeworlds of various Muslim societies with the claim and dogmatics of a universalist Islam? In this context, discussions about sacredness are representative here, because they are situated exactly at the interface between a local Islam on the one hand

and the need for universal validity on the other hand. Desplat's book is a contribution to studies on Muslim societies in Africa, on the ethnography of Ethiopia and the relations between religious practices, local power structures, and translocal networks.

DORSCH, HAUKE
"Indépendance Cha Cha": African pop music since the independence era
Africa Spectrum 45.2010:
Keywords: pop music, music, change and pop music

##Investigating why Latin American music came to be the soundtrack of the independence era, this contribution offers an over-view of musical developments and cultural politics in certain sub-Saharan African countries since the 1960s. Focusing first on how the governments of newly independent African states used musical styles and musicians to support their nation-building projects, the article then looks at musicians' more recent perspectives on the independence era.##

EPPLE, SUSANNE
The Bashada of Southern Ethiopia. A study of age, gender and social discourse
(Mainzer Beiträge zur Afrikaforschung 25)
Köln: Köppe Verlag 2010
291 pp., Euro 39.80; ISBN 3-89645-825-4
Keywords: Bashada, age among Bashada, gender, age-set societies, seniority

##Among the Bashada of Southern Ethiopia, individual misdeeds and wrong-doings are expected, especially when it comes to children and adolescents, as it is believed that misbehaviour is part of human nature. To prevent them from harming themselves and others, children, adolescents and adults have to be guarded, and guided, and also sanctioned by their age-mates and seniors. As unresolved conflicts are believed to bring about misfortune and cause disasters such as warfare, sickness or droughts, disturbed social relations are usually mended through social sanctions.
In her research Susanne Epple examines the specific social roles individuals achieve or are ascribed to during their lives. She looks at the specific modes of communication used to articulate, confirm and

strengthen social relations between children, adolescents, adults and elderly people of both sexes. In this context, she shows that the existing age-set organisation has an influence on all members of Bashada society. While the relationships between adult men as members of the different age-sets are clearly defined and interaction between them follows certain rules, the relations among children, adolescents and women follow the principle of seniority in a more general way. Besides giving a close insight into Bashada lives, Epple offers a new perspective on East African age-set societies.##

FABIAN, JOHANNES
Silesian memories. On recognizing contemporary African culture
Paideuma 56.2010:23-32
Keywords: language and anthropology, subjectivism

This is a rather personal account of Fabian's scholarly attitude and research: recognition, the subjective, language, medium and message, cultural identity and memory.

FUCHS, EVA
The impact of male migration on rural women in Morocco. A case study on gender and migration
(Interethnische Beziehungen und Kulturwandel 68)
Berlin: Lit Verlag 2010
109 pp., Euro 19.90; ISBN 3-643-10217-1
Keywords: migration, male migration, women and migration, gender and migration

##A lot of young Moroccan men migrate internally or abroad, searching for better living conditions for themselves and their families, leaving their wives, sisters and mothers behind. This study focuses on the impact of male migration on women, who are left behind in the rural area of Morocco. Taking into account that Moroccan households are based on patriarchal principles, which also define male and female roles, it gives a close analysis of Jorf, which is situated in the region of Tafilalet in southeast Morocco.##

FUEST, VERONIKA
Contested Inclusions: Pitfalls of NGO Peace-Building Activities in Liberia
Africa Spectrum 45,2.2010:3-33
Keywords: peace-building, civil society, grassroots agents, NGOs, conflict, development, participation

##In post-war situations, non-governmentat organizations (NGOS) feature highly in peace-building processes in their (perceived) capacities as both representatives of civil society and as grassroots agents to be employed in the reconstruction and transformation of society. As elsewhere, in Liberia, peace-building approaches include, first, international blueprints of representation that intend to empower groups generally perceived to be socially subordinate and, second, supporting traditional institutions considered social capital in reconciliation. Using the example of Liberia, this paper explores how in local conflict arenas, NGO workshops - the most popular mode of participatory intervention - are interpreted and appropriated by local actors; it highlights some fallacies and unintended consequences of inclusive procedures in practice and questions the support furnished to heads of gendered secret societies.##

GRÄTZ, TILO
Goldgräber in Westafrika
Berlin: Reimer Verlag 2010
239 pp., Euro 29.90; ISBN 3-496-02831-4
Keywords: gold diggers, frontier approach, labor organization, sociality and labor

Gold diggers in West Africa
Based on fieldwork in Benin, Burkina Faso, Mali, and Ghana between 1998-2003 the author discusses mainly the social and cultural situations of gold digging in these regions – social relationships emerging around this work, and how they are related to the major strategies of accumulation of these actors, which partly shows in the inclusion of strangers and the exclusion of members of the community. Another level is the interaction and everyday practice of the diggers vis-à-vis governmental and control institutions, the health dimension, social security, religious practice. The first chapter is about local contexts of gold digging in Northern Benin, then the labor organization of gold digging in the Atakora hills, juridical and political contexts, life worlds and forms of social integration, change and life histories after the gold boom in Northern Benin, and a comparison of

similarities and differences of case studies. In theoretically assessing these people the author finds the the notion of *frontier* useful, showing the openness of social arrangements in constituting these communities, as well as the slow solidification of social roles, structures, and norms.

GREINER, CLEMENS
Patterns of Translocality: Migration, Livelihoods and Identities in Northwest Namibia
Sociologus 60.2010:131-162
Keywords: migration, identity, translocality, rural and urban, urban lifestyle, transnationalism

##Social relations in Namibia's southern Kunene region are shaped by translocal patterns of migration, exchange and identity. Young people move to urban areas for schooling and work, older family members return to the countryside upon retirement to take care of the livestock and the rural homesteads. These movements are accompanied by remittances and resource transfers, critical for securing livelihoods in rural as well as in urban contexts. People experience movement between households from childhood on, and many migrants develop identities that combine rural and urban lifestyles. Still, the rural homes remain the symbolic, social and economic center for most migrants. Based on data from multi-sited fieldwork, this article examines the emergence and current patterns of migration, exchange and identity formation. The author outlines a translocal perspective and argues that, in order to deepen our understanding of these dynamics, it might be productive to borrow insights from recent studies of transnationalism.##

HAHN, HANS PETER
Urban Life-Worlds in motion: In Africa and beyond
Africa Spectrum 45,3.2010:115-129
Keywords: urban life worlds, mobility, urban-urban mobility, transnationalism, rural and urban, migration, innovative societies

##Although throughout the history of anthropology the ethnography of urban societies was never an important topic, investigations on cities in Africa contributed to the early theoretical development of urban studies in social sciences. As the ethnography of rural migrants in towns made clear, cultural diversity and creativity are foundational and permanent elements of urban cultures in Africa (and beyond). Currently, two new aspects complement these insights: 1) Different forms of mobility have received a new awareness through the concept of transnationalism. They are much more complex, including not only rural-urban migration, but also urban-urban migration, and migrations with a destination beyond the continent. 2) Urban life-worlds also include the appropriation of globally circulating images and lifestyles, which contribute substantially to the current cultural dynamics of cities in Africa. These two aspects are the reasons for the high complexity of urban contexts in Africa. Therefore, whether it is still appropriate to speak about the "locality" of these life-worlds has become questionable. At the same time, these new aspects explain the self-consciousness of members of urban cultures in Africa. They contribute to the expansive character of these societies and to the impression that cities in Africa host the most innovative and creative societies worldwide.##

JOCKENHÖVEL-SCHIECKE, HELGA
Soziale Reproduktion in den Zeiten von AIDS. Waisen und ihre Familien im ländlichen Tansania
(Ethnologie 34)
Berlin: Lit Verlag 2008
184 pp., Euro 19.90; ISBN 3-8258-1623-0
Keywords: Aids, orphans and Aids, foster children, poverty and Aids

Social reproduction in the era of AIDS. Orphans and their families in rural Tanzania
Due to the Aids epidemic in this area there are many orphans who are as part of a traditionals system accepted as foster children in extended families. The author analyzes this situation in the small coastal town of Pangani. The study includes the ‚voices’, opinions of the children: regarding their life-world, experiences of their parents’ death, and their expectations for the future. Chapters discuss poverty, gender relations and Aids in Tanzania, the town of Pangani is described, the notion of local life-worlds, schools, orphans and their care, life-words of HIV-positive women and their children, and finally, social reproduction in the times of Aids.

KESTING, MARIETTA
Politik und Sichtbarkeit in Johannesburg. „Wohlstandsgefängnis" und „Ghettoisierung" unter dem Primat der Sicherheitsfrage
(African connections in post-colonial theory and literatures 5)
Wien: Lit Verlag 2010
135 pp., Euro 19.90; ISBN 3-643-50114-1

Keywords: ghettoization, gated communities, nation-building, democratization, safety and space, space in cities, cities and space, visibility, Foucault, M.

Politics and visibility in Johannesburg. „Prison of wealth" and „ghettoization" and the priority of security
Kesting compares the Johannesburg neighborhoods of Hillbrow (poor, densely populated) and Dainfern (a gated community) to show two very different urban ways of life by starting from the „materiality of spaces" – to analyze cultural value concepts of a society, and she relates her study theoretically to Foucault's visibility, panoptism, etc. Thus, she discusses the differing generation of visibility „from above", and from below" which „creates a presence in the social-medial discourse of individuals and social groups" (19). In the second part of the book, exclusion and inclusion, political and societal implications are discussed, e.g., the „post-Apartheid situation characterized by visible and invisible lines of demarcation. She concludes that the establishment of gates communities, out of a desire for safety and separation, radically obstructs a South African process of nation-building and democratization, creating a deeply anti-democratic society.

KILIAN, CASSIS
Glimmering utopias: 50 years of African film
Africa Spectrum 45,3.2010:147-159

Keywords: film in Africa, feature films, movies, post-colonial film, utopia and film

##The history of African film began in the 1960s with the independence of the colonies. Despite all kinds of political and economic difficulties, numerous films have been made since then, featuring wide-ranging processes of consolidation, differentiation and transformation which were characteristic of post-colonial sub-Saharan Africa. However, these feature films should not merely be viewed as back references to specifically African problems. The glimmering fictions are imagination spaces. They preserve ideas about how the post-colonial circumstances should be approached. Seen from this perspective, the history of African film may be studied as a history of African utopias.##

KLEIN, THAMAR & KERSTIN HADJER (Eds.)
Sozialer Wandel im südlichen Marokko. Beiträge erster Feldforschungen
(Ethnologie 41)
Berlin: Lit Verlag 2010
121 pp., Euro 19.90; ISBN 3-643-10758-9
Keywords: social change, change, land rights, pottery, fieldwork, television

Social change in Southern Morocco. First fieldwork contributions
Students of anthropology, University of Cologne, present their first fieldwork experiences on: land right, pottery, dance, television – in Southern Morocco. They show social processes of transformation and the genesis of new forms of locality.
SACHOT, LEA-JEANNE et al.: Feldforschungsrealitäten im südlichen Marokko: Schwierigkeiten, Grenzen, Erfahrungen [Fieldwork realities in Southern Morocco: Difficulties, limits, experiences]
JUNCK, MANUEL: Ein Landrechtskonflikt im südlichen Marokko [A land dispute in Southern Morocco]
MIKISCH, TAIYA: Die Tänzerin betritt die Bühne: Aspekte des Wandels in der Repräsentation und Rezeption von Folkore [Aspects of change in the representation and reception of folklore]
WIPPERFÜRTH, PIA: Fernsehgewohnheiten und Fernsehrezeption von Frauen in Südmarokko [Habits of TV watching among women in Southern Morocco]
MEZGER, HEIDRUN: Töpferei im südlichen Draa-Tal: Wandel in Herstellungstechniken, Produktpalletten und Kommerzialisierungsprozessen von Tonwaren [Pottery in the southern Draa Valley]

KOSACK, GODULA
Den Geistern das Leben, den Menschen das Fleisch. Das Hühneropfer bei den Mafa in Kamerun
Curare 33,1/2.2010:105-109
Keywords: sacrifice, spirits, Mafa, earth sacrifice, poultry sacrifice

##The life for the spirits - the meat for the people. The Mafa'a poultry-sacrifice in Cameroun
All important acts of cult of the Mafa (North Cameroon) are accompanied by an animal sacrifice: a bull, a goat or a cock or hen. The latter is the most common, and the film will deal with this. Whether it is required to treat a sick person or it is part of an earth sacrifice, always the animal's life is dedicated to the spirits, who this way are honoured and nourished, while the humans are getting strength through eating the meat. (A film by Godula Kosack, 10 min).##

LUTTMANN, ILSEMARGRET
Fashion and fashion development in Africa – an introduction to the main research fields
Tribus 59.2010:100-135
Keywords: fashion development, meanings in fashion, globalization and fashion, tradition and fashion

##The 1990s saw the first forays into the study of African fashion-, mainly by American female scholars. This delving into a completely new topic introduced a broader view on social change in African related studies, particularly with regards to female agency and female subjectivities. In postcolonial West Africa women developed a very distinctive fashion system with fashionable styles which were very different to men's way of dressing. The article tries to give an overview of the main research findings with its main concern being the development of the so-called "African style" as a result of a popular cultural movement instigated by women. This style has several distinctive features whose meanings go far beyond the level of technical and aesthetical innovations. They embody broader essential cultural, moral and social values incorporated by women. Through fashion, women are articulating their idea of modernity while at the same time, using it as a means and strategy to reacting to globalization. The recourse to tradition is as central to their approach as the active albeit selective research of attractive global goods, technology and styles.##

LUTTMANN, ILSEMARGRET
Bustiers, pagne boulé und „Der Weg des Friedens" Modediskurse über Weiblichkeit, Identität und Politik in Abidjan
Anthropos 105.2010:503-537
Keywords: fashion, identity, femininity and fashion, world fashion, lifestyles, globalization of fashion

Bustiers, pagne boulé and „The way of peace" Fashion discourses on femininity, identity and politics in Abidjan
##Abidjan for long has been considered to be one of the most productive and progressive fashion centres on the African continent. One was wondering what would be the reactions in terms of output, style development, and meaning in times of political and economic crisis that the country is enduring since 2002. Furthermore, the processes of globalization have introduced significant changes with the tremendous quantities of textile imports from Asia and the intensified mediation of prestigious images of world fashion, western lifestyles, and role models of femininity. Surprisingly, Abidjan still turns out to to be a thriving city with a highly dynamic fashion sector whose trends and styles have won highest esteem in countries all over West and Central Africa. This study has two aims: On the one hand, it looks into the organization of production and circulation of fashion to get a better understanding of the local technical and material constraints and opportunities which prevail in this specific city. On the other hand, the focus is on the strategies of professional designers and urban women to cope with the influences of globalization i.e., the promises of and the limited access to the world market, the political and economic power of the West. Designers as well as women strive with local means to be part of the global world and to retain valuable local cultural values which are constantly redefined. Fashion and the invention of styles play a crucial role in articulating and assuming social changes.##

MAURER, ELKE REGINA
Fremdes im Blick, am Ort des Eigenen
(Sozioökonomische Prozesse in Asien und Afrika 12)
Freiburg: Centaurus Verlag 2010
422 pp., no price given; ISBN 3-8255-0768-8
Keywords: Masai, Samburu, sexuality, bi-national marriage, marriage, body and alterity, alterity and body, multiculturality, transcultural space, difference

Otherness in view, in the location of self
Maurer discusses the interaction of self and other, using the case of the movie *The white Masai*, because this film had a wide reception, making it fruitful for analysis. The content of a white woman's marriage with a Samburu is used as a frame to discuss this field. Maurer uses qualitative and quantitative data (applying sociological triangulation) – interviews, media information of various kinds. So she first presents her methodology, then the Samburu and their social structure, tourism in Kenya, then the book and following it the film. The next section deals with analysis and interpretation – the ‚power of images', Africa as a ‚dangerous continent', ‚black men' and sex, and analysis of reactions to the movie – sequence analyses of the contents/contexts/parts of the film. In this way ‚floor crossings' between cultures are described, transcultural encounters, multiculturality – how this actually takes place in the behavior of human beings.

MÖNCH, WINFRIED
Kamerun und Fernando Póo in Fotos von Hermann Harttmann. Ein Blick auf bemerkenswerte Bilder aus dem Ersten Weltkrieg
Tribus 59.2010:137-163
Keywords: Fernando Póo, museology, visual anthropology, photography, Harttmann, H., World War I

##*The Cameroons and Fernando Póo in photographs by Hermann Harttmann. A look at some remarkable pictures dating from World War I.*
The German colonial officer H. Harttmann (1885-1953) made photograph of the country and its people while on active duty in Africa before and during World War I. Of special interest are his pictures of the defeated remnants of what once had been the German colonial forces of the Cameroons interned in Fernando Póo from 1916 to the end of the war. The photographs are put in a historical context, dealing with the cultural and military conditions of the indigenous troops under his command. The German strategies applied by different commanders in East and West Africa are compared. Furthermore, some references are made to Harttmann's ethnographical work as well as to his military activities during World War II.##

NEVELING, PATRICK
Vom Nutzen der Geschichte, vom Wissen der Akteure und vom Nachteil der Multi-sited Ethnography. Welthandel, Wirtschaftskrise und Standortwettbewerb in Mauritius Anfang des 21. Jahrhunderts
Sociologus 60.2010:71-98
Keywords: economic crisis, agency, multi-sited ethnography, actor-centered perspective

##On the Uses of History, the Actor's Knowledge and the Disadvantages of Multi-sited Ethnography: Global trade, Economic crisis and the Politics of foreign direct investment in early 21st Century Mauritius
This article is concerned with reactions to an economic crisis, which struck the island state Mauritius when textile and garment manufacturers relocated their production to China, India and the African mainland. Based on the analysis of two public events which revealed strikingly different interpretations of the island's historical integration into global markets, a critique of "multi-sited ethnography" and its concept of globalisation and change is presented. Alternatively, this paper pleads for an actor-centered and historically informed understanding of change and continuity.##

OLDENBURG, SILKE
Under familiar fire: Making decisions during the "Kivu Crisis" 2008 in Goma, DR Congo
Africa Spectrum 45,2.2010:61-80
Keywords: crisis, conflict, violence, routinization, emergency, decision-making

##This paper explores the decision-making processes used by the inhabitants of Goma during the Kivu Crisis in October 2008. The paper's aim is twofold: After providing a short history of the October 2008 events, it seeks in the empirical part to distinguish and clarify the role of rumours and narratives in the setting of violent conflict as well as to analyse their impact on decision-making processes. As the epistemological interest lies more on the people who stay rather than those who flee, in the second part the paper argues that the practice of routinization indicates a conscious tactic whose purpose is to counter the non-declared state of exception in Goma. Routinization is defined as a means of establishing order in everyday life by referring to narratives based on lived experiences.##

PELICAN, MICHAELA
Umstrittene Rechte indigener Völker: das Beispiel der Mbororo in Nordwestkamerun
Zeitschrift für Ethnologie 135.2010:39-60
Keywords: indigenous rights, rights, leadership succession dispute, dispute of leadership, minority rights, Mbororo

Contested indigenous rights: The case of the Mbororo in northwest Cameroon
##This article discusses the problematic application of the concept of "indigenous peoples" to the African context. It critically considers the effects of international interventions aimed at reinforcing the realisation of the rights of indigenous peoples at the local and national level. The argumentation will be illustrated through a case of conflicting strategies of different actors in a leadership succession dispute in northwest Cameroon.##

POLL, SWENJA
Warum man sein Heim nicht verkauft. Wohnland im peri-urbanen Raum von Botswanas Hauptstadt Gaborone zwischen Ware und unveräußerbarem Besitztum
(Beiträge zur Afrika Forschung 43)
Berlin: Lit Verlag 2010
365 pp., Euro 29.90; ISBN 3-643-10210-2
Keywords: urbanism, peri-urban space, land use, property, commodity, living space, sex and misfortune, ritual sexual intercourse, sorcery, religion and land use, ritual and land

One does not sell one's home. Living space in the peri-urban area of Gabarone, Botswana capital, between commodity and unmarketable property
Tribal land in this area increasingly becomes a marketable commodity even though it is prohibited by juridical regulations. Neither the government nor state institutions are able to prevent such transactions. Simultaneously, local concepts of preventing disaster and suffering clearly limit the selling and other utilization of certain kinds of tribal land. The study, based on fieldwork, includes traditional views of various influences on the land where one lives, such as the negative influence of sexual intercourse other than of the couple living there in a house; it would create misfortune. Case descriptions and statements of informants add a dialogic dimension to the

study. Despite increased selling of land certain kinds are not sold: inherited land and land that has been ritually ‚impregnated' against sorcery.

RIEDERER, JOSEF
Die Metallanalyse der figürlichen Messingobjekte aus Benin im Ethnologischen Museum in Berlin
Baessler-Archiv 58.2010:107-120
Keywords: brass objects (Benin), museology, metal analysis

Metal analysis of figurine brass objects from Benin at the Ethnological Museum, Berlin
##A series of 56 bronze statuettes from Benin has been analysed by a emission spectrography and atomic absorption spectrometry. Since from already published analyses of memorial heads and relief plates it is obvious that there is clear relation between the composition of a brass object from Benin and its date of manufacture, there was a considerable interest to check whether the alloys used for the statuettes fit into this already established system.
The metal analysis of the statuettes showed that most of them have been made from a brass with very high amounts of zinc, which is a feature of products of the later phases of manufacture. But there are too some statuettes made of bronze or of a brass with low concentrations of zinc, characteristic for early objects. Besides the high concentration of zinc there are further arguments of a late production, like the high concentration of cadmium or the decrease of trace element concentrations, first of all of nickel and antimony.
With respect to characteristic features defined groups of statuettes, altar groups are rich in zinc, while statuettes of dignitaries contain less zinc. Among the statuettes of animals, those rich in zinc are frequent, but always there are a few examples with low concentrations of zinc, indicating an earlier origin.##

ROHRBACHER, PETER
Albert Drexel (18.6.1889-9.3.1977). Priester, Sprachwissenschaftler und Völkerkundler – Eine gesamtbiografische Würdigung
Anthropos 105-2010:555-566

Keywords: Drexel, A., linguistics, Africanist Institute, Missionary Academy, Institute of Racial Studies

Albert Drexel (18.6.1889-9.3.1977). Priest, linguist, and anthropologist – A biographical tribute
##The article commemorates the 120th anniversary of birth of Fr. Albert Drexel, today almost forgotten Austrian linguist, anthropologist, and an autodidact specialist in African languages. Drexel founded the „Africanist Institute" in Innsbruck in 1924, which later developed into "Missionary Academy", and finally, in 1935, into "Institute of Racial Studies." After the annexation of Austria by Hitler in 1938 Drexel was forced into exile in Liechtenstein. This study, based on little known archival sources, presents Drexel as an important contributor to the development of African studies and anthropology in Austria.##

SCHÄFER, MICHAELA
Weißes Gold Malischer Frauen oder: Was Entwicklung bedeuten kann. Karitébutter auf dem Weg in die Welt – vom „traditionellen" Fett zum Eliteprodukt
(Afrika und ihre Diaspora 8)
Wien: Lit Verlag 2010
199 pp., Euro 19.90; ISBN 3-643-50136-3
Keywords: shea butter, Karité, globalization, Bourdieu, P., Foucault, M., women and economy, cosmetics, agency

The white gold of Mali women, or: What development can mean. Shea butter on its way into the world – from „traditional" fat to elite product
Schäfer describes the changing utilization of the fatty substance gained from the fruit of the shea tree beyond local use: it is a process „from local to global and back". This fruit, the Karité nut is harvested and processed by women and is used for cosmetic and therapeutic purposes and in the food industry. Schäfer frames her topic with Bourdieu's theory of practice (fields of practices of development and transnational interaction) and Foucault's discourse analysis is utilized by analyzing legitimizing ascriptions, justifications and discourses for development – all of these are visible in the practices of the actors. Finally, repercussions of this process of ‚internationalization' of this product are traced back in the local field. The study is based on fieldwork and there are 24 persons interviewed.

SCHRAMM, KATHARINA
Sankɔfa-Interpretationen: Schwarze Selbst(er)findung zwischen Vergangenheitsbezug und Zukunftsorientierung
Sociologus 60.2010:191-218
Keywords: self, Akan-chieftaincy, Sankɔfa, identity, slavery

##*Sankɔfa-Interpretations: Re-Inventing the Black self - past and future*
„The future lies in the past" or „You need to know your past in order to move forward" - this is how the *adinkra*-symbol *sankɔfa* is often interpreted. Originally closely linked to Akan-chieftaincy, the symbol is nowadays popularized far bevond its local context. *Sankɔfa* has become a key reference for a positive interpretation of the past and an appreciation of tradition and it is consequently appropriated aesthetically as well as politically - both in a national as well as increasingly in an African-diasporic context. However, in diasporic understandings, *Sankɔfa* refers to yet another past, namely, to the complex history of slavery, which is connected to the question of black identity and belonging. The article traces these diverse appropriations in political, religious, cultural and consumption-oriented spheres. It asks about the specific connections that are drawn between past, present and future and seeks to understand the various notions of history and historical consciousness that go along with different understandings of national as well as black identity. These questions are discussed with reference to Haile Gerima's film „Sankɔfa" as well as to recentp developments in Ghanaian cultural politics and tourism.##

STEINBRINK, MALTE
The role of amateur football in circular migration systems in South Africa
Africa Spectrum 45,2.2010:35-60
Keywords, football, soccer, amateur football, migration systems, circular migration, labor and migration, rural-urban continuum, urban and rural, networks

##This article explores the significance of amateur football for the changing patterns of circular migration in post-Apartheid South Africa. Even after the end of Apartheid, the abolishment of the migrant labour system has not brought a decline of circular migration. The state-institutionalised system has merely been replaced by an informal system of translocal livelihood organisation. The new system fundamentally relies on social networks and complex rural-urban linkages. Mobile ways of life have evolved that can be classified as neither rural nor urban. Looking into these informal linkages can contribute to explaining the persistence of spatial and social disparities in "New South Africa". This paper centres on an empirical, bi-local case study that traces the genesis of the socio-spatial linkages between a village in former Transkei and an informal settlement in Cape Town. The focus is on the relevance of football for the emergence and stabilisation of translocal network structures.##

STRECKER, IVO
Ethnographic chiasmus. Essays on culture, conflict and rhetoric
(The Hamar of Southern Ethiopia V)
Berlin: Lit Verlag 2010
400 pp., Euro 29.90; ISBN 3-8258-7858-0
Keywords: Hamar, fieldwork, chiasmus, ethnography, rhetoric, war and peace, peace, self, knowledge, belief

##The essays assembled in this volume are shaped by conditions – both enabling and constraining – that can perhaps best be described as an „ethngraphic chiasmus". This expression refers to the surprise and reversal of position that are characteristic of fieldwork, and it attends to the fact that trans-cultural understanding comes about as a meeting, touching, or „crossing". Chiasmus also pertains to the relationship between culture and rhetoric in general. Culture structures rhetoric, rhetoric structures culture. Both are co-emergent. In order to elucidate this process, ethnography has to focus on the manifold modes of rhetoric through which culture-specific patterns of thought and action are created.## The essays in the book deal with the rhetorical creation of culture and self; rhetoric of war and peace; the rhetorical articulation of knowledge and belief. There are indexes of themes, dramatis personae, places and peoples, and authors.

THUBAUVILLE, SOPHIA
Die Wandernde ist eine Kuh. Lebenswege von Frauen in Maale, Süd-
äthiopien
(Mainzer Beiträge zur Afrikaforschung 22)
Köln: Köppe Verlag 2010
233 pp., Euro 36.80; ISBN 3-89645-822-3
Keywords: women, Maale women, agency of Maale, lifecycle of Maale women

The wandering one is a cow. Lives of women in Maale, Southern Ethiopia
Based on fieldwork mainly in 2006 this study on the life cycle of Maale women shows how their lives are marked, strenghtened and guided, and the importance of numerous rules of avoidance accompanying every phase of life. The description includes tensions between traditional avenues of action (agency) and changing life patterns, resulting from far-reaching change in Maale society. The description includes many statements of interviewees (of altogether 56 interviews), there are many photographs and drawings, maps, and a number of stories illustrating Maale culture.

THE AMERICAS

BIEKER, ULRIKE
Warriache in Temuco? Kommunikation von Ethnizität bei Mapuche in einer südchilenischen Stadt
Indiana 27.2010:269-295
Keywords: Mapuche, Warriache, urban Mapuche, ethnicity

Warriache in Temuco? Communication of ethnicity among Mapuche in a South Chilean city
##When considering urban indigenous people in Chile, attention is paid mostly to those living in the capital, Santiago de Chile, where nearly half of the indigenous population lives. The new ethnonym Warriache has been developed in order to denominate the urban Mapuche. Even so, there are many indigenous people, mainly Mapuche, living in the southern cities of Concepción, Temuco or Puerto Montt, who have been disregarded as such until recently. In my article I focus on the communication of ethnicity in the city of Temuco by means of food and poetics. Both aspects may be useful in describing the differences between the situations of urban people in the capital and the south, and in considering the significance of rural indigenous culture.##

BJERREGAARD, LENA
Pre-Colombian hairnets in the Museum of Ethnology, Berlin
Baessler-Archiv 58.2010:39-51
Keywords: hairnets, pre-Colombian hairnets, museology

##The Museum of Ethnology in Berlin has a collection of very delicate plant fiber hairnets. According to this study, they were made on the Central coast of Peru to around 14-16th century, and were used by both male and female weavers (although maybe not exclusively). A few of the nets are of camelid fiber but most are made of fine plan fiber yarns – i.e. *Furcraea Andina* (related to Agave). Most of the nets have intricate knotted patterns made in technique somewhat similar to *tatting*. About one third of the nets are painted with shellfish purple and a few with Indigo – mixed with a binding media. The nets are almost all from Pachamac, and they entered the museum in the beginning of the 20th century.##

CLADOS, CHRISTIANE
Tocapus in „loser Formation" im Mittleren Horizont, Peru: Federhut M 32205 des Linden-Museums, Stuttgart
Tribus 59.2010:164-179
Keywords: tocapus, headdress analysis, museology, artifacts

##*Middle Horizon Tocapus arranged in disconnected rows: Headdress M 32205 of the Linden-Museum, Stuttgart*
A feathered bi-convex headdress of unknown provenance in the Linden-Museum, Stuttgart, likely dates to the Middle Horizon based on an analysis of its central motif. This paper examines iconographic representations from different time periods to provide a relative date for the Stuttgart artifact and to clarify its original function. Special attention is given to the meaning of the central motif, which might be derived from realistically represented depictions or codified representations of Middle Horizon tocapus.
The headdress is covered with tiny feathers of turquoise, orange, and black on a yellow background. The feathers come from the throat of the Paradise Tanager, as well as from multiple species of parrots, and were attached to the fabric after the weaving was completed. Three horizontal rows of dice-like motifs decorate the headdress. The central motif consists of a square with four dots in that is repeated in three different color combinations around the headdress (Fig. 1).
The headdress originally might have been part of the artificial head of a mummy bundle similar to South Coast examples that are still preserved. Bi-convex headdresses are very common in Wari and Tiwanaku cultures, but also are seen on Nasca ceramics (Fig. 3) and according to Heidi King (personal communication), on Late Moche ceramics as well. Tiwanaku IV phase portrait vases and Wari stone and metal figurines (Pikillaqta) each show highly ranked men with this particular type of headdress (Figs. 2 and 4). Patricia Knobloch suggests that "[... I these particular depictions represent agents belonging to the Tiwanaku social sphere [...] ".
The central motif of the headdress, a square with four dots, also is found on a Middle Horizon 2A effigy vessel from the Denver Art Museum. In this case, the motif is combined with trophy heads (Fig. 5). Other closely-

related motifs include diagonal double motifs with two rings (Figs. 6 and 7) and four dots (Figs. 8 and 9).##

DREXLER, JOSEF
Das „Säen von Macht": Kosmovision zwischen politischer Ökologie und Lebenspraxis
Zeitschrift für Ethnologie 135.2010:23-38
Keywords: political ecology, ecology and politics, cosmovision, practice and ecology, land rights, Nasa, ethics of nature, shamanism

The „sowing of power": cosmovision between political ecology and lived practices
##In their struggles for land rights, territory and natural resources indigenous peoples of Latin America refer to their native cosmovision and ecological world-view. The ecological cosmology of indigenous peoples of the modern world system, however, is a dissonant juxtaposition, co-existence and drifting apart of local norms, concepts and practices dealing with "nature". Using the example of the Nasa (Páez) of the Columbian Andes, the following considerations investigate the theme of political ecology under the perspective of indigenous resistance. Thus the political ecology of the Nasa develops in the field of a multiplicity of lived practices, of a normative "cosmovision" - propagated by the Indigenous Regional Council of Cauca CRIC who conceives cosmovision as daily life practices that imply an indigenous cosmocentric ethics of nature - and a strategic apparatus of power. The revolutionary culturalist politics of the CRIC defines territory as a political-religious space and conceives shamanistic spirit as resistance of culture.##

EICHENBERG, ANDREA
Zu Gast bei Cigana Sara. Einige Überlegungen zur Symbolik des Candomblés
Cargo. Zeitschrift für Ethnologie 30.2010:41-47
Keywords: Candomblé, tsiganology, myths

Being a guest of Cigana Sara. Reflections on the symbolism of Candomblé

Eichenberg takes her participation in the festival of the Cigana Sara in Cachoeira, Bahia Brazil in 2008 to discuss Candomblé and questions of tsiganology.

GROTEHUSMANN, DIETER
Religion und Riten der Aymarà. Feldforschungen in der Region um den Titicacasee in Bolivien und Peru
(Religionen in der pluralen Welt. Religionswissenschaftliche Studien 10)
Berlin: Lit Verlag 2010
369 pp., Euro 29.90; ISBN 3-643-10493-9
Keywords: Aymarà, rituals of Aymarà, religion of Aymarà, mission, Christian mission, ,cosmovision' of Aymarà

Religion and rites of the Aymarà. Fieldwork in the area around Lake Titicaca in Bolivia and Peru
The author, a Protestant theologian and historian of religion, presents the „foundational concepts of Andine cosmovision" (in the case of the Aymarà), based on his fieldwork when he was in La Paz as a priest for seven years. Hence, the pretext is a chapter on Spanish mission, its history, partly of atrocities, and their theological counsel (e.g. on sexuality, the devil, afterlife...). Most of the book is devoted to „Aymarà cosmovision", their view of the human being, space and time, levels of the cosmos, agrarian and cyclical rituals and their specialists, life-cycle and healing rites, and rituals in the contested field between indigenous religion and Christian demands. In some cases (cosmovision of Aymarà and Spaniards, goddesses: Pachamama and Mary) the author attempts comparisons. The final chapter deals with rituals of death and afterlife.

KAMMLER, HENRY
Kulturwandel und die Konkurrenz der Religionen in Mexiko. Nahuas in Guerrero zwischen der Herrschaft der Winde und der Macht des Wortes
(Religionsethnologische Studien des Frobenius-Instituts Frankfurt am Main 5)
Stuttgart: Kohlhammer Verlag 2010
368 pp., Euro 59.80; ISBN 3-17-021154-4
Keywords: competition of religions, change, Nahuas, cultural change, religion and change, conversion, migration

Cultural change and the competition of religions in Mexico. Nahuas in Guerrero between the rule of the winds and the power of words
Kammler describes the interrelationships of cultural change with religious affiliations among three neighboring and variously structured village communities in the Mexican state of Guerrero. The focus is on the fact that although the three share similar general conditions of existence and similar cultural heritage, they nevertheless show different ways in designing their own modernity. Kammler asks if certain processes of change, such as decisions for or against a religious conversion, can be traced to local life practice which includes border-crossing migration. Religious fragmentation is taken as a sign that the traditional reservoir of collective convictions, i.e. a common myth as a source of meaning in life, is not sufficient any more to deal with problems of an accelerated cultural change.

LAMBERG, SIGRID
Subsistenzökonomie in Nicaragua. Perspektiven in einer sich transformierenden Gesellschaft
Frankfurt/M.: Brandes & Apsel 2010
296 pp., Euro 24.90; ISBN 3-86099-668-3
Keywords: industrial agricultural production, substistence, agriculture, WTO, Free Trade Zone, development

Subsistence economy in Nicaragua. Perspectives in a transforming society
Nicaraguan agrarian infrastructure ranges from industrial production to substistence. Lamberg inquires into the influence liberalization has on agriculture, coming from the WTO, or as a result of the ratification of the Central American Free Trade Zone treaty. She confronts this development with detailed description of realities of life of the indigenous *comunidades* living in the autonomous areas of the country, and who apply subsistence forms of production – asking whether this subsistence-oriented economy can be a realistic alternative to „development" measures, or whether this may be ‚social romanticism'. Lamberg describes the historical and political background, and for her fieldwork in 2007 uses a mix of qualitative social science research (document analysis), semi-structured interviews, and participant observation. The last chapter includes details about the Región Autónoma del Atlántico Norte.

LUTTER, MARK
Zur Erklärung von Diffusionsprozessen. Das Beispiel der Einführung staatlicher Lotterien in den USA
Zeitschrift für Soziologie 39.2010:363-381
Keywords: diffusion processes, lottery, event history, statistics, organizations

##Explaining Diffusion: The introduction of state lotteries in the USA
This paper examines the determining factors in the diffusion of state lotteries as a process of policy innovation. After more than 100 years of prohibiting them, individual states in the US began to establish lotteries in the 1960s. Statistical event history analysis is used to show that the adoption and diffusion of state lotteries depends on fiscal, political, and regional factors of competition as well as on normative factors of social legitimization. Two further arguments are developed, discussing, for one, an advanced model of regional diffusion that views the regional effect as dependent on the ideological-institutional context and, secondly, analyzing time dynamics in the diffusion process to show how initial explanatory factors change over time. In general, the findings indicate that the institutional environment shapes the diffusion of organizations.##

STOLLE, NIKOLAUS
Heinrich Moritz Hebenstreit und seine Sammlung aus dem indigenen Nordamerika
Baessler-Archiv 58.2010:7-37
Keywords: Hebenstreit, H.M., material culture, museology, Cumanha, collectors

Heinrich Moritz Hebenstreit and his collection from indigenous North America
##Descriptions of material culture and knowing how and when objects were being collected in indigenous North America is essential to understanding their age, distribution, style, use and meanings – not only in the history of collecting, but regarding the evolution of material culture itself. The following paper deals with the Hebenstreit collection, which was acquired by the Berlin Royal Kunstkammer in 1840, and is now part of the Ethnologisches Museum, Berlin. On one hand the attempt is made to describe the collection's history and its collector, and on the other hand this work will focus on describing in particular the indigenous objects, which are ostensibly of „Cumanha" origin.##

STEINEN, ULRICH VON DEN
Expeditionsreisen am Amazonas. Der Ethnologe Karl von den Steinen (1855-1929). Mit einem Geleitwort von Mark Münzel
Köln: Böhlau Verlag 2010
166 pp., Euro 19.90; ISBN 3-412-20618-5
Keywords: Steinen, U. v.d., travelogues, discovery, tattoo

Expeditions along the Amazon River. The anthropologist Karl von den Steinen (1855-1929
The physician von den Steinen was one of the most well-known scholarly travellers of his time, exploring then unknown areas around the source of the Xingu River, a southern tributary of the Amazon where he met indigenous peoples. The present biography includes his travels and life, showing von den Steinen as strong opponent of racism and political strivings for occupation. He was one of the first to bring home specimens for collections and diaries, but also a new image of man: the human roots and development out of an ancient culture. The second part of the book deals with Steinen's travels in Oceania, the Marquesa Islands.

TONGERLOO, ALOIS VAN & MICHAEL KNÜPPEL
Zu den „Aztekischen Studien" Willy Bangs
Indiana 27.2010:229-236
Keywords: Aztecs, Bang, W., linguistics, turkology, Nahuatl

On the „Aztec Studies" of Willy Bang
##Hardly anyone knows today that the turkologist Willy Bang had briefly dealt with the Nahuatl language in the 1890s, when he published a short paper on this issue under the pseudonym „W. Baligny".##

TRENK, MARIN
„Der Apfel ist die Banane des Indianers" Zur Gastroethnologie des nordöstlichen Nordamerika
Anthropos 105.2010:355-367
Keywords: gastro-anthropology, food, anthropology of food, Moravian Brethren, Delawares, Iroquois, culinary traditions, fusion food, crossover cuisine

„The apple is the banana of the Indian" On the gastro-anthropology of northeastern North America
##The anthropology of food has made little use of historical source materials. Eighteenth-century North America boosts a vast number of sources rich in ethnographic detail, particularly the notes and publications of the missionaries of the Moravian Brethren. This article attempts to reconstruct the native cuisines of the Northeast and their transformations, focusing mainly but not exclusively on the Delawares and Iroquois. Their foodways were not tribal or "ethnic" but part of a broader culinary pattern or regional cuisine. Although structurally simple, they were more varied than commonly acknowledged. Everyday dishes were differentiated from festive ones, but a culinary differentiation into "high" and "low" cuisine was unknown. Some foreign foodstuffs crossed the culinary frontier and were incorporated into native foodways. But no fusion food or crossover cuisine emerged. Only with the adoption of sugar, tea, coffee, and chocolate culinary stratification did start. These imported "drug-foods" became prestige and luxury foods, thus anticipating similar colonial and postcolonial processes in the centuries to come.##

WANGENHEIM, HUBERTA VON
Der gesellschaftliche Diskurs des Phänomens der médium unidad, *einer besonderen Form der Wahrnehmung, im Kontext afrokubanischer Religionen*
Curare 33,1/2.2010:72-89
Keywords: religions, psychopathology, possession, healing, extrasensory perception, senses, médium unidad, prophetic dreams, trance, enchanted perception, spirits

##*The social discourse of the phenomenon of* médium unidad, *a form of perception in the context of Afro-Cuban religions*
The phenomenon of *médium unidad* plays an important role in Cuban society as a particular way to experience the world. The term designates a specific, from a western point of view extraordinary capacity of perception that includes various facets such as premonitions, hearing voices, seeing something that does not exist materially in the visual field, prophetic dreams and states of possession-trance. I call these experiences of sensual perception enchanted perception ("beGeisterte Wahrnehmung"). They are lived and treated as such caused by spirits, who transmit truthful and meaningful messages. This occurs due to the influence of Afro-Cuban religions on the social conception of reality. The concept of *médium unidad*

represents a socially constructed practice of perception, which exhibits an alternative to the usual treatment of comparable phenomena in western-scientific contexts. Especially in psychiatry they are classified in general terms as psychopathologies. This articles examines the treatment of these phenomena in Cuban society using spiritistic women's life histories in Havana.##

ZUCKERHUT, PATRICIA
„Sin maíz vamos a morir" Mais im Zentrum von Ökonomie, Religion und Identität
Anthropos 105.2010:57-71
Keywords: gendered violence, violence, corn, personhood, identity, Nahua

Corn in the center of economy, religion, and identity
##Corn is of central meaning for Nahuat-speaking people of Sierra Norte, Puebla, Mexico. It is an integral part of personhood und closely related to ideals of harmony, of (gender)cooperation and (hierarchical gender) complementarity. The article explores the relation of disturbed male harmony, resulting from missing opportunities, to adequate corn production in the context of globalization. This may lead to increased illegitimate gendered violence by men. Besides, it will also be demonstrated how new forms of cooperation and complementarity between husband and wife are developed and may contribute to less hierarchical and less violent gender relations.##

ASIA

ALEX, GABRIELE
Medizinische Diversität im postkolonialen Indien. Dynamik und Perzeption von Gesundheitsangeboten in Tamil Nadu
(Berliner Beiträge zur Ethnologie 21)
Berlin: Weißensee Verlag 2010
375 pp., Euro 34,-; ISBN 3-89998-181-0

Keywords: medical diversity, healing, traditional healing, Unani, Siddha medicine, Ayurveda, medical anthropology, subaltern groups, emic perspective, health seeking behavior, Vagri, Mutturaja, Paraiyar

Medical diversity in postcolonial India. Dynamics and perception of health care opportunities in Tamil Nadu
Alex presents a medical anthropological approach on healing systems and traditions, medical care structures and concepts of health and illness in Tamil Nadu. It is an introductory book using case studies by adopting the emic perspective of subaltern groups on these health systems of rural Tamil Nadu, and by relating them to indigenous concepts and categories of health and illness. This includes non-formalized healing practices which are not represented in official statistics regarding health. This ethnographic part serves as context for the analytical part which aims to contextualize and analyze the valuation and acceptance of the various health care opportunities in rural Tamil Nadu, based on quantitative and qualitative data. The chapters introduce the castes involved (Vagri, Mutturaja, Paraiyar), theoretical issues of medical anthropological perspectives, the health system in India and concepts of health and illness in Tamil Nadu (i.e., Tamilian notions, a typology of causes). This is followed by a description of the ‚medical landscape': governmental and non-governmental institutions, pharmacies, folk medicine, pujaris, and various specialized healers. The next chapter is devoted to the professionalization of traditional medicine connected with the Vagri. Ten brief case studies discuss the health seeking behavior of individuals, and the last chapter evaluates preference of the various institutions/healers frequented, based on interviews. The appendix contains questionnaires, diagrams, photograph, a glossary, etc.

BÜNTE, MARCO
Demokratie in Südostasien auf dem Rückzug?
Asien 116.2010:40-62
Keywords: democracy, retreat of democracy, authoritarian regimes, economic development

##*Is democracy in crisis in Southeast Asia?*
The article gives an overview over the status of democratization in southeast Asia by looking at established democracy indices such as the Freedom House data and Bertelsmann Transformation Index. After mapping the regime types of Southeast Asian states, the article analyses the state of consolidation in southeast Asia's young democracies with Linz/Stepan's model of democratic consolidation. The article shows that democracy has received serious setbacks only in Thailand (and to a certain extent also in the Philippines), whereas Indonesia's democracy has gained maturity in recent years. These developments are reflected in constitutional consolidation, political party development and the reform of the militaries of the region. The prospects for democratization are quite gloomy, since most of the authoritarian regimes in the region lack the conditions considered conducive for democratization, such as economic development, a vivid and active middle class or vigorous working class. External influences also favour the status quo and do not support democratization.##

BUSS, ANDREAS
Die Völkerrechtstheorie und das regionale, buddhistische Gewohnheits-recht Südostasiens. Der Fall des Tempels von Preah Vihear
Internationales Asienforum 41.2010:193-213
Keywords: customary law, law, international law, municipal law, Buddhist law

The theory of international law and the regional Buddhist customary law of Southeast Asia. The Case of the temple of Preah Vihear
##The issue of the Preah Vihear case (1962) in international law has long been debated and even today creates tensions between Thailand and Cambodia. This article analyses Siam's position within the international law structure in the early twentieth century, when the issue arose it also reminds the reader of a tradition in international law theory which does not consider international law and municipal law as essentially different, and on this basis it then suggests that there is a regional (Buddhist) customary law and regional principles in Thailand and the surrounding regions of

Southeast Asia that could profitably have been considered by the International Court of Justice.##

FALLER, SUSANNE
Devatās aus Himachal Pradesh. Nordindische Metallarbeiten im Linden-Museum
Tribus 59.2010:180-191

Keywords: masks, artifacts, museology, devatās, mohrās, Śiva, Devī, Brahmā, Viṣṇu, Vajrayāna Buddhism

##*Devatās of Himachal Pradesh. North Indian metal works in the Linden-Museum Stuttgart*
The Linden-Museum Stuttgart owns a very impressive collection of masks of Himachal Pradesh. These are called *devatās* or *mohrās*. The mohrās are normally fixed in groups upon a palanquin (*ratha*) and are kept in their own shrines. For certain festivals they are carried across the mountains and bow to each other on the *maidān* (place for festivals). The *mohrās* of the Linden-Museum can be identified as Śiva, Devī and a snake-deity (*nāga*). One of the masks could be regarded as Narasiṃha.
Exceptional is a votive plaque of the *trimūrti* Brahmā, Viṣṇu and Śiva. Viṣṇus mace is here interpreted as a spear which is typical for the region south of the Sutlej. Very unusual is the lion throne (siṃhāsana)Viṣṇu is placed on. This is most likely a local syncretism as the lion is a symbol of a sovereign and the Śākya clan into which the Buddha was born. In the Western Himalayas we can find Buddha Śākyamuni, Mañjuśrī, Tathāgata Vairocana and even Gaṇeśa seated on a lion throne. Also the peacocks might represent the symbolic animals of the Tathāgata Amithāba since Vajrayāna Buddhism is practised in the surrounding areas.##

FERDIN, MARIUS, STEFAN GÖRLITZ & STEFFEN SCHWÖRER
Water Stress in the Cauvery Basin, South India - How current water management approaches and allocation conflict constrain reform
ASIEN 117.2010:27-44

Keywords: water management, conflict and water, irrigation

##This article presents insights on the state of water management in the Cauvery basin in South India and the ongoing interstate dispute concerning the allocation of the Cauvery's water between the riparian states Karnataka and Tamil Nadu. A lack of multi-level, intersectoral, and participative approaches on the one hand have led to inadequate conditions in water management and water use. On the other hand, the conflict between the two states on water allocation cannot be resolved due to strong reluctance and non-compliance by the states and a highly politicized debate. We identify some clear correlations between inadequate internal water management at the state level and the interstate dispute: the ongoing conflict constraining modernization of the system in the basin is used to justify-non-action in irrigation-management reform and ties up state resources as well. Additionally, the current water-management approach does not provide for a mechanism to address the concerns and demands of stakeholders, nor does it promote dialogue between them.##

GAIL, ADALBERT
Structure and decor – The development of the serpent motif in Orissa sacred architecture
Tribus 59.2010:192-201
Keywords: serpent motif, artifacts, museology, nāgas

##From Nepal's omnipresent Viṣṇu reclined on the coils of Śeṣa, who represents the primeval waters, down to Sri Lanka's beautiful nāga stelae and Nāgarājas, that are the foremost guardstones of Buddhist Stūpas (dagoba), the serpent motif is of utmost importance in the whole South Asian realm.

Nowhere, however, more impressive than in Orissa the nāga motif forms a structural type of embellishment of both Hindu temples and Buddhist monasteries. More often than not it appears in the vertical recesses of walls. Earlier, the nāgas and nāgīs, each encircling his or her respective pilaster, erect their anthropomorphic busts on the lower parts of the shafts, while their tails elegantly climb upwards (exempli gratia Mukteśvara). Later, their movement is turned, caused by aesthetic reasons, as it seems (exempli gratia Rājrānī).

The finest blossom of nāga decor is represented by the great sun temple of Koṇārka. The nāgas now form erotic couples, entwined, each pair encircling only one pilaster. Finally even the amount of Nāgas on one pilaster is enlarged up to six creatures, anthropomorphic and zoomorphic shapes artistically mixed.##

GERHARZ, EVA
Endlich, Frieden? Lokale Sichtweisen von Ethnizität, Geschlecht und Entwicklung im Norden Sri Lankas
Internationales Asienforum 11.2010:33-55

Keywords: peace, gender, development, Eelam, Liberation Tigers, LTTE, actors, local actors

Peace at last? Local views of ethnicity, gender, and development in Northern Sri Lanka

##Taking the current situation characterised by the defeat of the Liberation Tigers of Tamil Eelam (LTTE) by the Sri Lankan military forces in May 2009 as a starting point, this article looks into the potential prospects for peace. The main part is based on an empirical case study conducted in the northern peninsula of Jaffna, where the LTTE lost their stronghold in the mid-1990s. The subsequent occupation of Jaffna by the Sri Lankan military forms the point of departure for an analysis of reconstruction and development efforts after the cease fire of 2002. Based on a detailed analysis of shifting gender relations this article argues first that the interrelatedness of gendered and ethnic relations with regard to the construction of local „culture" produces meaningful markers for demarcation. The second focus relates to local perspectives on the state as an actor in development and reconstruction. The article highlights that local actors' negotiating of the potential role of both the state and the LTTE are ambivalent and embedded in constructions of sameness and difference. The article concludes by shedding light on recent developments and Sri Lanka's future perspectives.##

GIERSDORF, STEPHAN & AUREL CROISSANT
Zivilgesellschaft und kompetitiver Autoritarismus in Malaysia
Asien 116.2010:80-102

Keywords: civil society, authoritarianism, NGOs, social movements, elites, autocratic elites, coercion, cooptation

Civil society and competitive authoritarian in Malaysia

##This article analyses the development of civil society in Malaysia under competitive-authoritarian rule. Applying the concept of historical institutionalism, institutional legacies will be identified which have been and still are of great influence on the structures and functions of Malaysian civil society. The study shows that civil society changed profoundly since

1957, with regard to its structures and functionalities. An ethnically segmented civil society, based on religious, cultural and functional interest groups, has been replaced by a civil society which is built upon NGos and social movements which are well-connected with other opposition actors. The article argues that civil society groups are increasingly emerging as challengers for the autocratic elites. Nevertheless, by using coercion and co-opting parts of the opposition, the autocratic elites continue to keep the civil society in check in order to stabilize their autocratic rule. However, the use of coercion and cooptation is restricted due to the regime's competitive character, thus producing a structural, functional and operative limited civil society.##

GRAEFE, STEFFEN
Der neue radikale Hinduismus. Indien im Kampf der Kulturen
Berlin: Lit Verlag 2010
323 pp., Euro 29.90; ISBN 3-643-10472-4
Keywords: Hinduism, radical Hinduism, Hindu nationalism, nationalism and fundamentalism, fundamentalism, alterity, philosophy and nationalism, fatalism

The new radical Hinduism. India in the clash of civilizations
The author classifies his study of Hindu nationalism as a study in the history of philosophy, a critical analysis of the history of ideas concerned, and he thus attempts to show the effects of mythically enhanced and simultaneously corrupted ideas on real-political ideologies until today. He finds fundamentalist driving forces and ideologies in Hindu nationalists aiming at the separation of otherness, and he interprets the Hindu nationalists' attempts to press indigenous tradition into the framework of the national idea as an adaptation of western nationalists and social darwinists of the 19th century. The chapters discuss the question of the ‚clash of civilizations' in relation to the critical method of an intercultural philosophy, Kant and the complex of morals, then Indian history and ‚fatalism', traits of fatalism in the Mahābhārata – and the Bhagavadgītā, followed by the question of whether Kṛṣṇa's fight in this text might be a ‚Djihad'. The last chapters deal with aspects of fragmentation in ancient India, and finally Hindu nationalists of more recent times. The conclusion deals with the ‚cosmopolitical essence of the Indian tradition'.

GRIMM, REINMAR
Kurzer Bericht über die deutsche Indien-Expedition 1955-58, insbesondere über ihre völkerkundliche Ausbeute
Tribus 59.2010:203-219
Keywords: German India-Expedition 1955-58, Maydell, G.A. Baron von, ethnographic artifacts, Gonds, Garos, Jain altar

Short report of the German India-Expedition 1955-58, particularly its anthropological gain
##The German India-Expedition 1955-58, lead-managed by Gustav Adolf Baron of Maydell, was probably the last "universal" collecting expedition which started from Hamburg, namely by order of the Zoological Institute and Museum. The main focus of the expedition was on the field of zoology, botany and ethnology. Baron of Maydell collected scientific material for quite a number of further museums, institutes and scientists within and outside Hamburg and here especially for the Zoological Garden, Wuppertal, the Linden-Museum, Stuttgart, and the Overseas Museum, Bremen.
In the field of ethnology mainly articles of daily and commercial use should be collected. Even though the ethnological yield purely quantitatively did not come up to the zoological and botanical, the expedition collected altogether 233 ethnological objects of daily, commercial and cultic use (from still very aboriginal ethnic groups, especially the Gonds and Garos) which were distributed among three well-known museums. The highlight of the ethnological collection turned out to be the Jaina altar which was turned over to the Linden-Museum.##

GUGLER, THOMAS K.
The new religiosity of Tablīghī Jamā'at and Da'wat-e Islāmī and the transformation of Islam in Europe
Anthropos 105.2010:121-136
Keywords: Islamic mission, mission, Sufis, ‚Sunnaization', pilgrimage, terrorism

##The Islamic missionary movements Tablīghī Jamā'at, Da'wat-e Islāmī, and Sunnī Da'wat-e Islāmī share, in varying degrees, a Sufi background, and preach a peaceful Islam. At the same time, terrorists involved in the bombings in Europe since 20021 regularly visited mosques associated with these movements, especially the Tablīghī Jamā'at. The "Islamic project" of the three movements is the "Sunnaization" – that is, the reshaping and reconstruction - of the daily routine and the individual markers of identity based on the examples of the Prophet and the Salaf (the pious ancestors) as portrayed in the Hadīth literature. This so-called "apolitical" Sunnaization can be understood as the privatization or individualization of political re-Islamization.##

GUGLER, THOMAS K.
Pakistan nach den Islamisten: Transformationsprozesse innerislamischer Rivalität und Populärislamismus
Asien 117.2010:58-78
Keywords: Islamism, religious extremism, jihad, sectarian jihad, regional jihad, global jihad, political Islam, neofundamentalism

Pakistan after the Islamists: Transformation processes of internal Islamic rivalry and popular Islamism
##Islamic interpretations heavily impact on political culture and practice in Pakistan. Religious extremisms, which repeatedly have been resulting directly from state politics in Pakistan, become at times dominant to an extent that they threaten to undermine the foundations of state and society. Radical groups engage in several jihads: internal sectarian, regional jihads in Afghanistan and India, in addition to global jihads against the West. Analyzing transformation processes of politicized religion, introducing institutional structures and political dynamics, the article portrays the main trends in political Islam in Pakistan, striving to understand how the failure of political Islamist projects fostered the popularity of new post-Islamist neofundamentalisms.##

HABICH, SABRINA
Corporate Social Responsibility in der chinesischen Textilindustrie: Unternehmerische Verantwortung chinesischer Prägung
Asien 114/115.2010:88-113
Keywords: Corporate Social Responsibility (CSR), responsibility and labor, industry and responsibility, textile industry, labor conditions, companies and responsibility

Corporate Social Responsibility in the Chinese textile industry: Corporate Social Responsibility Chinese style

##Within the past couple of years Corporate Social Responsibility (CSR) has enjoyed growing attention by China's public and private sector. When the concept was introduced to China by western companies and international organizations in the 1990s, the Chinese government at first regarded CSR as a hindrance to its national economy. Only recently did the government start to apply the concept for domestic as well as international purposes. This paper analyses the introduction of CSR to an industry highly affected by the concept's emergence - namely the Chinese textile and apparel industry. Apart from laying bare how CSR is applied in the Chinese context, the paper explains how the concept is integrated into the industry's restructuring process and how the Chinese government is attempting to handle the challenge of poor working conditions in the industry by passing the problem on to the private sector and the society. At present, CSR only has a limited influence on the amelioration of working conditions in China. While positive effects that have been achieved in several companies should be acknowledged, they should not divert the gaze from a still urgently needed construction of effective regulation.##

HAUG, MICHAELA
Poverty and decentralisation in East Kalimantan. The impact of regional autonomy on Dayak Benuaq wellbeing
(Sozioökonomische Prozesse in Asien und Afrika 13)
Freiburg: Centaurus Verlag 2010
292 pp., Euro 25,-; ISBN 3-8255-0770-1
Keywords: poverty, decentralization, autonomy, wellbeing, Dayak, poverty, well-being

##With the implementation of regional autonomy Indonesia passed one of the most rigorous decentralisation reforms throughout Asia. These far reaching reforms generated a variety of new opportunities in East Kalimantan, but with high costs in the social and natural environments. This book explores the impacts regional autonomy had on the well-being of the Dayak Benuaq – one of the diverse indigenous groups of East Kalimantan. It describes the Dayak Benuaq's own perceptions of poverty and well-being, documents processes of ongoing social, political and economic change, and demonstrates how they are intertwined with decentralisation. The ethnographic case studies of three Dayak Benuaq villages show that decentralization is not – as often assumed – automatically pro poor. Instead, it is the respective bargaining power of local actors which determines the outcomes of decentralisation.

Introducing a newly developed model to capture the multidimensionality of poverty and the trade-offs among the different aspects of well-being, this study contributes to research on poverty and well-being. It further provides insights into the local dimensions of decentralisation and contributes to a better understanding of recent processes of socioeconomic change in Borneo. This case study offers valuable insights into questions of importance scholars as well as policy makers concerned with poverty and the impact of decentralisation on local livelihoods.##

HÖFER, REGINA
Kultbild oder Art Object – Zur Bedeutung indischer Ästhetik für eine zeitgemäße Ausstellungspraxis zwischen Kolonialmuseum und White Cube
Zeitschrift für Ethnologie 135.2010:79-98
Keywords: museology, exhibitions, colonialism and museums, art objects, white cube, Indian art, global art, aesthetics

Cult Image or Art Object - Implications of Indian Aethetics for Modern Curating among Colonial Museum and White Cube
##The paper examines the nature of traditional Indian aesthetics and possible consequences and implications of exhibiting Indian art in the West. In this context the distinction between religious and modern resp. contemporary or present-day Global Art plays an important role. Against the background of the British colonialisation, the paper furthermore explores the effects of the influence of Western aethetics and its influence on Indian art and museum practices. The author opts for the equality of Indian and Western aesthetics and point out peculiarities of, but also similarities in both systems.##

HOOD, MADE MANTLE
Triguna. A Hindu-Balinese philosophy for Gamelan Gong Gede music
(KlangKulturStudien 2)
Berlin: Lit Verlag 2010
476 pp., Euro 49.90; ISBN -3-8258-1230-0
Keywords: musicology, Gamelan music, Hinduism and music, triguna, Hinduism, guna concept

##This book combines ethnography, philosophy and musical analysis for an in-depth look into the social context and musical praxis of gamelan gong gede, the largest gamelan orchestra of bronze gongs and percussion on the island of Bali. The Hindu-Balinese notion of three human qualities called triguna serves as an interpretive framework for categorizing the musical repertoire according to both widespread religious knowledge and more esoteric wisdom.## The first part describes origins and ownership of orchestras in five districts, the second the repertoire which makes a discussion of the guna concept necessary. The author discusses the three gunas according to Indian textual sources, Balinese resources, and finally the Balinese Prakempa manuscript, which describes pre-20th century Balinese gamelan traditions. The next chapter interprets the repertoire according to the three gunas (satwam, rajas, tamas), and the last part of the book analyzes the repertoire musicologically, followed by detailed appendices.

LEHMANN, NICOLE MANON
Sama und die ‚Schönheit' im Kathak. Nordindischer Tanz und seine ihn konstituierenden Konzepte am Beispiel der Lucknow-gharānā
(KlangKulturStudien 4)
Berlin: Lit Verlag 2010
671 pp., Euro 49.90; ISBN 3-643-10252-2
Keywords: dance, Kathak, beauty and dance, Hinduism, rasas

Sama and the ‚beauty' of Kathak. North Indian dance and its constituating concepts in the case of the Lucknow gharānā
Starting point is the question how ‚beauty' is constituted in the North Indian Kathak dance. And Lehmann traces her major thesis, that *sama* carries ‚beauty' as *rasa* in Kathak dance by involving and considering a number of influences and factors:
- social concepts of the *gharānā* and *gurū* teachings;
- religious/philosophical constructions of the cosmos, of time, of the myth of the god *Kṛṣṇa* and *Rādhā*;
- historical contexts such as the *bhakti*-movement with its *Rāslīlā* theater;
- Muslim and British influence;
- the rhythm analysis of *tāla*, *laya*, and the musical fix point of *sama*;
- the *nāyikā* role- and *abhinaya* movement concepts;
- the aesthetics theory of *rasa* and *bhava*.

Thus, cultural background and numerous contexts are included, the teaching itself, praxis at the Bathkhande Music Institute of Lucknow, the dance itself (notions and sequences of dance with explanations), roles, analysis of movements, dance as the manifestation of cosmic order, and analysis of rhythm. The appendix as numerous photographs of dance positions, and gestures.

MARCINKOWSKI, CHRISTOPH
Shi'ite identities. Community and culture in changing social contexts
(Freiburger sozialanthropologische Studien 27)
Wien: Lit Verlag 2010
285 pp., Euro 24.90; ISBN 3-643-80049-7
Keywords: Shi'ite identities, Islam, Twelver Shi'ites, terror and Islam

##The current political events surrounding the Iranian nuclear crisis, the precarious situation in Lebanon, as well as the still unsettled fate of Iraq have resulted in a renewed interest in the Shi'ite dimension of Islam among political observers. This volume covers the phenomenon of political assertiveness among contemporary Shi'ite Muslims in the Middle East, as well as among converts in southeast Asia. It argues that Shi'ite identities are often based on local cultural heritage and history and are – contrary to what is usually assumed by the wider public – not to be considered monolithic.## Concepts and practices of the „Twelver Shi'ites", who make up about 80% of Shi'ites worldwide, are presented, followed by their attitudes toward the Qur'an. The Buyid period is described as an age of classical Shi'ite scholarship, then Iran's ambitions are discussed, also Iraq and the ‚Lebanese connection'. Then, Shi'ism in the diaspora in Southeast Asia is presented, and the postscript discusses prospects for a ‚Catholic Shi'ite project'.

MENNIKEN, TIMO & SUSANNE SCHMEIER
Regionale Kooperationsstrukturen am Mekong. Die institutionalisierte Regelung von Konflikten um natürliche Ressourcen
Internationales Asienforum 41.2010:215-242
Keywords: regional cooperation, conflict management, water conflicts, natural resources, resources conflicts

Regional structures of cooperation on the Mekong. The institutionalized mediation of conflict over natural resources

##The rapid economic growth and development which characterizes the mainland Southeast Asian countries in the Mekong River Basin is based largely on the exploitation of natural resources with the Mekong River and its natural resources playing the most important role. However, the increasing exploitation of these natural resources and the growing pressure on these due to population growth and other developments in the river basin are likely to lead to problems among the different resource users. This will pose particular problems due to the transboundary nature of the river - with actions of one riparian state necessarily affecting other states. Hydropower development and climate change are most liable to cause conflicts of interests. This paper focuses on the Mekong River Commission (MRC) as an institutionalized body for river basin management and analyzes its contribution to the resolution of the aforementioned problems and to the mitigation of water resources-related conflicts.##

MEYER, HARALD
Zyklische Geschichtsauffassung und Zeitkritik: Das essayistische Vermächtnis des japanischen Bestsellerautors Shiba Ryōtarō (1923-1996)
Internationales Asienforum 11.2010:103-124
Keywords: Ryōtarō, S., cyclical history, apprehensions of time

Cyclical views of history and criticism: The essayistic heritage of the Japanese Bestseller author Shiba Ryōtarō (1923-1996)
##With some 200 million copies of his various publications sold to date Shiba Ryōtarō must indeed be one of Japan's best-selling authors. His œvre includes not only a vast number of historical novels, but also numerous essays on Japanese history, lectures and recorded discussions with other writers and scholars. This paper focuses on Shiba's legacy, especially his late essays on a number of aspects of Japanese modern history and various cycles of historical development. His critical views about Japan's severe financial crisis during the bursting of the so-called "bubble economy" are also included. At the end of his life, Shiba tended to be rather pessimistic about the future of his country. Looking back from today by quoting several comments by some of Shiba's most concerned readers also helps us get a better understanding of the present status of public opinion in Japan.##

MICHAELS, AXEL ET AL. (Eds.)
Grammars and Morphologies of Ritual Practices in Asia. Including an E-Book-Version...
(Ritual dynamics and the science of ritual 1)
Wiesbaden: Harrassowitz 2010
591 pp., Euro 98,-; ISBN 3-447-06201-5
Keywords: ritual, grammar of ritual, semiotics and ritual, Vedic ritual, fire sacrifice, Daoism, Vedism, Buddhism, healing rituals, Batō fire offering

##Held in Heidelberg from September 29 to October 2, 2008 by the collaborative research center SFB 619 "Ritual Dynamics", the international conference "Ritual Dynamics and the Science of Ritual" assembled most of the leading experts on rituals studies and more than 600 participants for the purpose of reassessing the traditional subject in view of the latest research. The results, which are presented in five volumes, are pathbreaking for future transcultural, interdisciplinary and multimethodical research on rituals. The convention was marked by the broad range of disciplines and the corresponding diversity of methods. It embraced a great variety of topics in terms of cultural geography and spanned a time horizon from antiquity to the present. The proceedings show how broadly the term ritual can be defined, as well as the conditions, modes and functions of ritual actions in different cultures of the present and past.##

MICHAELS, AXEL: The Grammar of Rituals
HOUBEN, JAN E.: Formal Structureand Self-referential Loops in Vedic Ritual
SARAOGI, OLGA SERBAEVA: When to Kill Means to Liberate: Two Types of Ritual Actions in Vidyāpīṭha Texts
MISHRA, ANAND: On the Possibilities of a Pāṇinian Paradigm for a Rule-based Description of Rituals
MICHAELS, AXEL (in collaboration with JOHANNA BUSS): The Dynamics of Ritual Formality: The Morphology of Newar Death Rituals
GALEWICZ, CEZARY: Inscribing Scripture Through Ritual: On the Ritual Cycle of Trisandhā
GAENSZLE, MARTIN: Grammar in Ritual Speech: The Use of Binomials in Rai Invocations
BRONKHORST, JOHANNES: Ritual, Holophrastic Utterances, and the Symbolic Mind
HEESTERMAN, J.C.: The Development and Impact of Ancient Indian Ritual

WILKE, ANNETTE: Basic Categories of a Syntactical Approach to Rituals: Arguments for a "Unitary Ritual View" and the Paraśurāma-Kalpasūtra as "Test-Case"

LUBIN, TIMOTHY: Ritual Self-Discipline as a Response to the Human Condition: Toward a Semiotics of Ritual Indices

FREEMAN, RICH: Pedagogy and Practice: The Meta-pragmatics of Tantric Rites in Kerala

SMITH, FREDERICK M.: Historical Symmetry and Ritual Asymmetry: The Interrelations between Vedic Ritual and Temple Construction in Modern India

STAAL, FRITS: A Theory of Ritual: The Indo-Iranian Fire Offering

PUETT, MICHAEL: Ritualization as Domestication: Ritual Theory from Classical China

GENTZ, JOACHIM: "Living in the Same House": Ritual Principles in Early Chinese Reflections on Mourning Garments

MEYER, CHRISTIAN: Interpretations of Confucian Ritual („li") in Chinese Scholarly Discussions in the Eleventh Century

RAZ, GIL: Ritual Theory in Medieval Daoism

TSAI, JULIUS: Mutation or Permutation? A Ritual Debate in Tang-Song Daoism

DOLCE, LUCIA: The Contested Space of Buddhist Public Rituals: The *shunie* of Tōdaiji

OUCHI, FUMI: Buddhist Liturgical Chanting in Japan: Vocalisation and the practice of attaining Buddhahood

TRIPLETT, KATJA: Esoteric Buddhist Eye-healing Rituals in Japan and the Promotion of Benefits

BUTLER, M.A.: Ritual Specialists and Collective Agency in Song Dynasty China

ATKINS, PAUL S.: The Stages of *Seppuku*: Performing Self-execution in Premodern Japan

ANDERSEN, POUL: The life of images in Daoist ritual

LOMI, BENEDETTA: The Iconography of Ritual: Images, Texts and Beliefs in the Batō Kannon Fire Offering

OBERDIEK, ULRICH
Die Agravāls in Rajakshetra (Kumaon Himālaya). Lebensstile, Habitus, Ökonomie und „Puritanismus" in einer Händlerkaste
(Indus. Ethnologische Südasien-Studien 14)
Berlin: Lit Verlag 2010
515 pp., Euro 49.90; ISBN 3-643-10556-1

Keywords: Agravāls, merchant castes, caste system, Puritanism, purity, lifestyle of castes, jāti, trading castes, sacrifice, vegetarianism, ritualism, genealogy, mythology, sexuality, animal sacrifice, Weber, M., Hinduism, social control, control behavior, norms of castes, guṇa, Marriott, M., identity

The Agravāls of Rajakshetra (Kumaon Himālaya). Lifestyles, habitus, economy and „Puritanism" in a merchant caste
This is a detailed ethnography of the merchant caste population of Agravāls living in a market town of the Himalayan foothills in Kumaon, and it is a problem-oriented study of „Puritanism". History, mythology (three foundational texts are translated from Hindi), and major cultural traits of this caste/jāti (rituals, festivals, exchange, economy, social control, segregation, purity/impurity...) are presented, based on fieldwork (1995/96) and on textual sources. It is a problem-oriented study as well, inquiring whether there is a so-called „puritanical" lifestyle in this caste, as has been claimed for „higher" Hindu castes in general by numerous authors. These authors are presented in detail (Carstairs, Srinivas, Manisha Roy, A. Bharati, A. Jha...), and theoretical models of „Puritanism" other than historical Puritanism are presented (E. Gellner, Waardenburg...). Cultural contents of historical Puritanism are analyzed first as a basis to deal with behavior in the case of the Agravāls in a second step.

Hence, in the field situation, the concept of purity, based on textual concepts of guṇa and its present occurance in belief and behavior is dealt with, which coincides with the work of McKim Marriott. Then, 19 cases or instances of what may be understood as „puritanical" behavior are described and analyzed against the theoretical background, and cultural-biographical sketches of a number of persons of this caste are included throughout the study. Altogether, roughly fifty families have been researched, amounting to 94 individual persons, including 28 women. Results show that there is behavior and belief among some persons, comparable to what may be called „puritanical", but motivations (ethics) and „mechanics" of such behavior differ significantly from that of historical Puritans as described by Max Weber and others: Motivation, or theology inspiring such behavior is of a different kind. Another result is a „devaluation" of the assumption of a kind of homogeneous group identity of this caste – instead, individual and family-dominated identity has been found. This agrees with a theoretical trend departing from seeing castes as homogeneous units, and with an increasing focus on persons in anthropological studies.

OELSCHLÄGEL, ANETT C.

Plurale Weltinterpretationen und Transdifferenz: Dominanz- und Inter-aktionsmodell in der alltäglichen Praxis der West-Tyva in Süd-Sibirien
Zeitschrift für Ethnologie 135.2010:305-336
Keywords: worldviews, Tyva, dominance, interaction, plural worldviews, agency, model-switching, transdifference

##*Plural world interpretations and transdifference: Models of dominance and interaction in everyday practice of the West Tyvans in South Siberia*
This article analyses the flexible way of handling plural models of world interpretation in West Tyvan daily practice. Based on fieldwork in the Republic of Tyva (Russian Federation) in 2004/2005, it is part of a research project that led to a dissertation submitted to Leipzig University in 2010. At least two models of world interpretation were identified. Both exist as realities of equal value but can structurally be differentiated as "model of dominance" and "model of interaction." The first stresses the human dominance over the environment, seen as a series of more or less passive objects of human agency," the second emphasizes the "Interaction in a world enclosing humans and consisting of both human and non-human subjects." Both models are coherent systems and belong in equal degree to the repertoire of knowledge, behaviour and acting of West Tyvan agents. To them, these models count as equal and mutually contradictory. The models compete and oppose each other, but form a continuum within a single person to the effect that the human agent is constantly positioning himself, depending on situation and context. The empirical material demonstrates that West Tyvans use these models in various ways - replacing, complementing and mixing them according to their needs in specific contexts.##

PARK, HEE SEOK
Die Metamorphose des Schamanismus. Die Transformation der altreligiösen Kultur zum Medium des Protestes im heutigen Südkorea
Internationales Asienforum 41.2010:323-345
Keywords: shamanism, religious culture, protest and religion, politics and protest

The metamorphosis of shamanism. The transformation of the old religious culture to a medium of protest in present-day South Korea
##The 1970s and the 1980s saw a great surge in the protest movement in the Republic of Korea. In its course student activists and intellectuals unexpectedly turned to traditional culture as their source of inspiration. Folk culture, for example shamanism, long considered a distant relic of the past, found a new focus. This paper addresses one question in particular: how an old religious culture, which had been suppressed as "superstitious" in the public sphere, resurfaced through the protest movement. In this context two aspects are examined based on writings from this period: what implications did shamanism hold for those in protest circles; and what function did this belief system perform for the protest movement. It is shown that three distinctive features of shamanism were brought into prominence in the literature examined. In the final analysis it is argued that the protest movement utilised the old religious culture as a means to distance itself from the authoritarian regime.##

PLATZ, ROLAND
Die Welt des Wayang in Berlin
Baessler-Archiv 58.2010:121-130
Keywords: wayang puppets, museology, puppets of wayang

The world of the Wayang at Berlin
The Berlin Museum of Ethnology has a large collection of all kinds of *Wayang* puppets from Java and Bali. Most of them originate from the 2nd half of the 19th century. The focus of this article is on the Javanese *Wayang kulit* puppets. They were mainly sold to the museum by two Dutch collectors, Pleyte and Masthoff in the end of the 19th century. No curator so far published the fact that these puppets of the Berlin collection are smaller than the average figures from Java. In quality terms they are less refined than the usual puppets of that time. In fact they are called *wayang kaper*, puppets used for training the *dalang*, the puppet master.

Nevertheless this collection seems to be one of the biggest wayang kaper sets in Western museums. The Balinese puppets, however, and especially the large wayang golek puppet collection, some of them dating back to the middle of the 19th century, are high quality objects. As a joint project, one young Javanese *dalang* came in 2009 to the Berlin Museum of Ethnology to work on the Javanese *wayang kulit* collection. Parts of the *wayang* puppets will be seen in the future in the Humboldt Forum. The last time they were displayed was more than 10 years ago.##

POSER, ALEXIS TH. VON
Blasius Jong – Ein ethnographischer Nachruf auf einen allwissenden Informanten aus Papua-Neuguinea
Baessler-Archiv 58.2010:131-138
Keywords: Jong, B., informants, Kayan, fieldwork

Blasius Jong – An ethnographic obituary of an omnicient informant from Papua New Guinea
Starting from the life-history of Blasius Jong, a recently deceased cultural expert from Kayan village at the North Coast of New Guinea, the article discusses the role of the omnicient informant in fieldword contexts. The notion of an all-encompassing cultural expertise from one single representative of a social group has long been out of fashion in anthropological discourse. Considered to be a post-Durkheimian relic in early ethno-science, the omniscient informant might be re-introduced from an unexpected direction: from the study people themselves. In the case of Jong, the members of Kayan society relied on one version of everything considered traditional and historical: the version of this old man. When the ethnographer arrived, he was immediately associated with this expert and the resulting publication is considered to cover ,Kayan culture' for all members of the group. The implications of this on politics of knowledge and the problem of the fixation of one version in time all part of the discussion.##

PREIS, NINETTE
Train friends. Frauenfreundschaften im indischen Nahverkehrszug Ladies Special
Heidelberg: Draupadi Verlag 2010
228 pp., Euro 24,-; ISBN 3-937603-47-6
Keywords: train friends, female friendships, friendship

Train friends. Women friendships in the Indian local train ‚Ladies Special'
Preis describes commuting women (of the „middle class") meeting in this local train in the Mumbay area: in what contexts friendship emerges, what this means, what the women talk about, what they do during this time, and activities of such friends beyond the train. Friendship as defined by Preis includes ‚informality, voluntariness, expansion in time, mutual exchange and values'. Preis asks what the basic values of such relationships are, and what this means in terms of research on friendship in anthropology and neighboring disciplines. The author found conviviality and spending time together as central values.

SCHIMMELPFENNIG, MECHTHILD
Tuskiise und ihre Ornamentik zwischen Tradition und Westorientierung im modernen Kasachstan. Eine kulturanthropologische Untersuchung
Baessler-Archiv 58.2010:91-106
Keywords: wall hangings, museology, westernization, felt artifacts, textiles

Tuskiis and their embroidery between tradition and western orientation in modern Kazakhstan. A cultural-anthropological study
##Traditional wall hangings of Kazakh yurts, called *tuskiis*, are documented since the middle of the 19th century. Since then they underwent various phases of change in their outer appearance and in the attributed meanings. This contribution analyzes this change departing from the 19th Century wall hanging out of felt produced communally and for personal use to individually embroidered wall hangings and finally textiles of manufacturers of the 1980s which today are sold as national emblems to tourists. The main questions regard the social and cultural conditions and meanings of this process of change.##

SCHORKOWITZ, DITTMAR
Geschichte, Identität und Gewalt im Kontext postsozialistischer Nationsbildung
Zeitschrift für Ethnologie 135.2010:99-160
Keywords: identity and violence, violence, post-socialist nation-building, nation-building

History, identity, and violence in postsocialist nation-building
##With the breakdown of socialism in Eastern Europe in the late 80s and its earlier decline in the wake of Deng Xiaoping's ambitious reforms preparing the People's Republic of China for the global market, images of the past are utilized for power accumulation by various national elites. The comeback of national ideas in postsocialism went along with the replacement of communist dogmas, a radical shift in ideological paradigms and a concurrent re-emergence of ethnicity leading to an increasing ethnicization and confessionalization of the social sphere. These processes not only reinforce existing tendencies of regionalism in multinational states paving the way for administrative-territorial reshuffles and nationalistic-based segregations in peripheral regions. They often also veil the extent to which nativist and post-colonial movements are frequently intertwined in their strife for cultural and political sovereignty.
The paper examines some of these aspects with regard to Krasnodar in Southern Russia, a region neighbouring Abkhazia, the second case study, representing one of the two renegade entities that declared independence from Georgia after the South Ossetia War in August 2008. Moldova being still a member of the CIS, as Georgia was before the war, is finally discussed concerning the Transnistrian conflict. Showing different path dependencies, these regional conflicts present transformation courses with similar results: Consensus making among ethnically divergent groups is accompanied by cultural delimitation that confronts the 'own' with the 'other'. Historical and social memories are employed in this process as tools for an 'otherization' profiled identity building, as are language, faith and other cultural markers. Violence is used in this context as a catalyst to push the development, triggering incalculable dynamics that lead to further escalation. Ethnic cleansing in Georgia and Moldova, in Azerbaijan and Armenia, in Lhasa, Urumchi, and recently in Osh gives proof to the suitability of this mechanism that cut off century old socio-cultural ties within few days.##

SCHRÖDER, FREDERIKE & MICHAEL WAIBEL
Urban Governance of Economic Upgrading Processes in China: The Case of Guangzhou Science City
Internationales Asienforum 41.2010:57-82

Keywords: urban governance, economic upgrading, economic growth, non-state actors, actors, mega-cities

##Facing intense inter-city competition, urban development strategies in China's metropolises require constant adaptation. To enhance economic strength and competitiveness, the shift from labor-intensive manufacturing towards modern service and high-tech industries is actively promoted on all policy levels. This change is particularly enforced in the mega-urban region of the Pearl River Delta (PRD) which for a long time has been known as the world's factory. The main argument of this paper is that advancement along the value chain and the implementation of industrial upgrading processes require new institutional arrangements. Following an analytical governance approach, these are described taking the development of Guangzhou Science City as case study. Innovative components such as strategic urban planning and the increasing inclusion of non-state actors in development processes indicate a shift towards more market-oriented modes of urban governance. These modes allow the municipal governments a higher degree of flexibility and the implementation of a pro-growth-regime within a highly competitive urban environment.##

SCHRÖTER, SUSANNE (Ed.)
Christianity in Indonesia. Perspectives of power
(Southeast Asian modernities 12)
Berlin: Lit Verlag 2010
420 pp., Euro 29.90; ISBN 3-643-10798-5

Keywords: Christianity, Protestantism, mission, delelopment, Catholicism, iconoclasm, monotheism, religion and mission, Islam, colonialism, ethnicity, pluralism

This book is based on the conference by the same title at the Goethe University of Frankfurt, Germany in 2003.

##Indonesia is a multicultural and multireligious nation whose hetero-geneity is codified in the state doctrine, the Pancasila. Yet the relations between the various social, ethnic, and religious groups have been problematic down to the present day. In several respects, Christians have a precarious role in the struggle for shaping the nation in the aftermath of the former president Suharto's resignation and in the course of the ensuing political changes Christians have been involved both as victims and perpetrators in violent regional clashes with Muslims that claimed thousands of lives. Since the beginning of the new millennium the violent conflicts have lessened, yet the pressure exerted on Christians by Islamic fundamenialists still continues undiminished in the Muslim-majority regions. The future of the Christians in Indonesia remains uncertain, and pluralist society is still on trial. For this reason the situation of Christians in Indonesia is an important issue that goes far beyond research on a minority, touching on general issues relating to the formation of the nation-state.##

SCHRÖTER, SUSANNE: Christianity in Indonesia: An Overview
SCHUMANN, OLAF: Christianity and Colonialism in the Malay World
WARNK, HOLGER: Missionaries and Malay Schoolbooks: The American Mission Press/Methodist Publishing House, 1890- 1928
STEENBRINK, KAREL: The Power of Money: Development Aid For and Through Christian Churches in Modern Indonesia, 1965-1980
SCHRÖTER, SUSANNE: The Indigenization of Catholicism on Flores
CORBEY, RAYMOND: „Thou Shalt Have no Other Gods Before Me!" Iconoclasm on the Christian Frontier
RODEMEIER, SUSANNE: Tradition and Monotheism in Eastern Indonesia
BRÄUCHLER, BIRGIT: Religions Online: Christian and Muslim (Re)presentations in the Moluccan Conflict
BARTELS, DIETER: The Evolution of God in the Spice Islands: Converging and Diverging of Protestant Christianity and Islam in the Moluccas During the Colonial and Post-Colonial Periods
ARAGON, LORRAINE V.: Relatives and Rivals in central Sulawesi: Grounded Protestants, Mobile Muslims, and the Labile State
KOSEL, SVEN: Christianity, Minahasa Ethnicity, and Politics in North Sulawesi: 'Jerusalem's Veranda' or Stronghold of Pancasila?
NOORHAIDI, HASAN: The Radical Muslim Discourse on Jihad, and the Hatred against Christians
MAGNIS-SUSENO, FRANZ SJ: Pluralism under Debate: Indonesian Perspectives

SKINNER, ALEXANDRA ET AL.
The Challenges of E-Waste Management in India: Can India draw lessons from the EU and the USA?
Asien 117.2010:7-26
Keywords: e-waste, export of e-waste

##This article examines e-waste management in India, identifying lessons and implications from e-waste management in the European Union and the United States which may influence or predict both strengths and obstacles to effectiveness in Indian e-waste regulation. India's new draft E-waste (Management and Handling) Rules are much more comprehensive than any US e-waste regulations and contain several similarities to ihe EU's current WEEE Directive. The inclusion of the EPR principle and the role of stakeholders in formulating the draft rules are both positive developments that are essential to address the e-waste problem successfully. Once in effect, however, the draft rules are likely to face many of the same obstacles to implementation and enforcement present in the EU and the US. Ultimately, until an international definition of e-waste is in place and the economic causes of illegal e-waste export and handling are addressed in all three entities, enforcing regulatory compliance and eliminating the health and environmental hazards related to e-waste dismantling in India will remain difficult.##

TRENK, MARIN
„Essen wie die Tiger". Aneignung und Ausgrenzung einer Regionalküche in Thailand
Internationales Asienforum 41.2010:243-267
Keywords: food, eating, ethnic food, Thai cuisine, culinary traditions, fish salad, identity, regional identity

„Eating like tigers". Appropriation and exclusion in a Thai regional cuisine
##Isaan, Thailand's northeastern region, has traditionally been margi-nalized and its Lao-speaking population still faces discrimination. But its regional culinary traditions have reccntly captivated all classes of Bangkok's food-conscious population. This article attempts to map the complexities of the nation's acceptance and the spread of Isaan's regional cuisine. Over the past 20 years a few Isaan dishes have been appropriated and adopted to Thai tastes. This culinary "Thai-ization" has "de-ethnicized"

and "de-regionalized" some local foods. These co-opted dishes are already considered to be part of the emergent national cuisine of Thailand. While some dishes have been accepted, others are still discriminated against, especially *plaaraa*, a non-pasteurized fish sauce, and the Carpaccio version of Isaan's iconic dish *laap*, a raw spicy minced meat or fish salad. Traditionally these types of dishes were rejected on cultural grounds but today national campaigns against certain Isaan foods are debated in terms of "health concerns", while serving the goals of national political integration. The people of Isaan react by developing a culture of resistance, turning some raw dishes into markers of regional identity. These local strategies are supported by global culinary trends (Sushi!) making Isaan food irresistible even in Bangkok's haute cuisine.##

TÜRK, ANDREAS
Christentum in Ostsumba. Die Aneignung einer Weltreligion in Indonesien aus praxistheoretischer Sicht
(Religionsethnologische Studien des Frobenius-Instituts Frankfurt am Main 6)
Stuttgart: Kohlhammer Verlag 2010
571 pp., Euro 79,-; ISBN 3-17-021548-1
Keywords: Christianism, world religions, practice (theory of), theory of practice, Bourdieu, P., performativity, mission, Protestant mission

Christianism in East Sumba. The appropriation of a world religion in Indonesia from the perspective of the theory of practice
The Christian religion has become a global phenomenon and presently shows its major dynamic in Africa, Latin America, and Asia. Türk presents a multi-faceted image of a local manifestation of this religion in Sumba, taking five practices (worship, home meetings, mission, burial, marriage) to explain how Christian belief becomes part of everyday life, and thus from something alien to the familiar, or own. Appropriating this world religion (or being converted) follows a „logic of practice" for which Türk utilizes Bourdieu. In this ethnographic context, the following Protestant groups are concerned: 1) Nederlandsche Gereformeerde Zendingsver-eeniging, in the 18th and 19th centuries; 2) the Gereja Kristen Sumba after the foundation of independent Indonesia in 1945; but there are Pentecostal groups active as well: Jemaat Pentakoste, or Kemaah Injil.

WAGENER, MARTIN
Institutioneller Autismus. Die ASEAN und der thailändisch-kambodschanische Grenzkonflikt
Internationales Asienforum 41.2010:169-192

Keywords: institutional autism, border conflict, ASEAN, conflict and borders, foreign policy, Preah Vihear temple

Institutional autism. The ASEAN and the Thai-Cambodian border conflict
##Southeast Asia ushered in a new era with the adoption of the ASEAN Charter in 2007 which entered into force a year later. At a time when ASEAN is transfirming itself into a legal entity, unprecedented skirmishes broke out between two of its members on the border of Thailand and Cambodia. The background of this confrontation is an old dispute linked to the ancient Preah Vihear temple. The International Court of Justice ruled in 1962 that the ruins belong to Cambodia but made no decision concerning the adjacent land. To this day, Bangkok and Phnom Penh are making competing claims over this 4.6 km^2 piece of land close to the border. The situation escalated when the Preah Vihear temple was designated a world Heritage Site in July 2008, following Cambodia's application to UNESCO. The upshot: several gun fights between October 2008 and June 2010 with at least eight soldiers killed. The contrast could not have heen greater: officially proclaimed institutional change and the use of military force by two member states. The conflict says a lot about Cambodian and Thai foreign policy. But above all it allows conclusions to be drawn about the proccss of regional integration in Southeast Asia. There can be no doubt that the gap between rhetoric and reality is widening. From a medical viewpoint, the patient, in this case ASEAN, can be described as suffering from "institutional autism".##

WEIGL, CONSTANZE
Reproductive health behavior and decision-making of Muslim women. An ethnographic study in a low-income community in urban North India
(Indus 15)
Berlin: Lit Verlag 2010
250 pp., Euro 29.90; ISBN 3-643-10770-1

Keywords: reproductive health, medical anthropology, Muslim women, fertility, contraception, family planning, abortion, Islam and reproduction

##As a consequence of the politicization of religion in India, the study of Islam in fertility is a highly sensitive issue. How do Muslim women make decisions relating to their fertility and practice of contraception? How do factors [such] as socio-cultural norms, socioeconomic constraints, national family planning policies, and Islamic legal tenants affect women's reproductive health behavior? This ethnographic study answers these questions by analyzing the local context, in which the lives of these low-income Muslim women are embedded. Theories and concepts of demography are also explored and critically reflected on.## This study, based on fieldwork in the Hazrat Nizamuddin Basti of New Delhi in 2007-8, explores choices, behavior and attitudes of women there, with regard to reproduction. So, women's agency is described, the context and infrastructure of the Basti is portrayed as well as the context of marriage, fertility, reproduction, lifestyle, etc. In this context values, women's health, contraception, abortion is studied on the basis of participant observation. The last chapter deals with these questions in the light of the Qu'ran and Islam in general. Among other findings, the study shows that fertility of these Muslim women is not higher than that of their Hindu neighbors, and that decisions clearly depend on general socio-economic situations they live in.

WEIGL, CONSTANZE
Empfängnisverhütung und Familienplanung muslimischer Frauen in Nordindien
Curare 33,1/2.2010:53-59
Keywords: contraception, family planning, Muslim women, reproduction, fertility, health care

##*Contraception and Family Planning Among Muslim women in Northern India*
This article examines the reproductive health behavior of Muslim women in Northern India. It is based on ethnographic research conducted in a low-income community in New Delhi/India. Contrary to common belief, women's reproductive choices and family planning in this community are not determined by local religious beliefs and practices. Instead they are influenced by a number of socio-economic constraints as well as governmental family planning policies and women's poor state of health. These factors result in a decline of fertility. This decline is linked to an increased access to biomedical contraceptive methods as well as women's

awareness of the latter. However, the introduction and availability of these contraceptive methods also create new problems, such as medical side effects and perceived health hazards.##

WERNING, RAINER
Programmierter Dauerkonflikt? Die Suche nach einem tragfähigen Frieden in den Südphilippinen
Internationales Asienforum 41.2010:303-322
Keywords: conflict, peace

A programmed permanent conflict? Searching for sustainable peace in the Southern Philippines
##The southern Philippines Mindanao, Basilan and Jolo in particular – is plagued with the longest-running conflict in Southeast Asia which has claimed the lives of approximately 150,000 people. Several attempts since the mid-seventies to ease the tensions have ended in deadlock, the latest being the thwarted signing of the so-called Memorandum of Agreement on Ancestral Domain (MoA-AD) in August 2008. This paper tries to explain the length of the conflict and its salient features. In particular, it deals with the interests pursued by the main protagonists and the factors leading to recurring internal frictions and divisions within the ranks of organized Moro resistance. It also sheds light on the prospects for the numerous NGOs and observers of the International Monitoring Team (IMT) stationed in the southern Philippines to ensure permanent peace in the region and to forge closer political as well as economic ties with neighboring Malaysia and Indonesia.##

WU, XIUJIE
Brotherhood considered – Responsibility and tensions concerning elderly support in North China
Sociologus 60.2010:219-240
Keywords: brotherhood, alliance, hierarchy, egalitarianism, extended case study, conflict, elderly support, Han-Chinese, kinship, anxiety

##The culture of the Han-Chinese designates brotherhood as a valuable form of alliance. Codes of behaviour towards one's brother(s) are ascribed in cultural norms. However, within the concept and practices of kinship, ambiguous borderlines of hierarchy and egalitarianism among brothers leave certain areas free for contesting individual interests. This article takes an extended case study of conflict between two brothers in their old age over their elderly support provisions to analyse how notions of brotherhood are re-shaped as Chinese peasants are confronted with serious social insecurity due to lower incomes and insufficient institutional arrangements for elderly support; how conventional concepts of hierarchy, equality, and fairness have been mobilised, interpreted in different ways to justify their own rights and rightness before the civil judgements of other viliagers and the verdicts of the juridical system. This case study directs the reader's attention to the different facets of societal transformation in the last three decades, which impact kinship arrangements, and accordingly caused immense individual anxiety.##

YALÇIN-HECKMANN, LALE
The Return Of Private Property. Rural life after agrarian reform in the Republic of Azerbaijan
Berlin: Lit Verlag 2010
225 pp., Euro 29.90; ISBN 3-643-10629-2
Keywords: private property, property, agrarian reform, rural poverty, poverty, privatization

What makes private property valuable, desirable, or workable? In this book, Lale Yalçın-Heckmann focuses on social and economic dimensions of private property after the agrarian reforms of 1996 in Azerbaijan. She looks at the kinds of land and cultivation strategies emerging in the decades after the fall of the Soviet Union and asks why rural households are often unwilling to cultivate the privatised land shares they have received for free, despite the threat and existence or rural poverty. Consideration is given to households that engage in cultivation and households that you do not – including households of internally displaced persons who were formerly excluded from privatisation but were nevertheless successful and eager cultivators. The author asks, how far does private property thrive it on its own, without the support of lucrative markets for the implementation of state-sponsored economic policies? Through the lens of economic anthropology she chronicles the historical legacy of authoritarian state structures and the contemporary micro- and macro-economic struggles that mark the politics of property after socialism.##

ZIMMERMANN, ASTRID ELISABETH
Raumkonzepte, soziale Organisation und Übergangsriten in der heutigen Mongolei
(Tunguso Sibirica 29)
Wiesbaden: Harrassowitz Verlag 2010
174 pp., Euro 48,-; ISBN 3-447-06152-0

Keywords: space concepts, passage rites, marriage, Ööld and marriage, post-socialism, ritual, nomads and ritual

Concepts of space, social organization and passage rites in present-day Mongolia
Central focus of this study is the description and analysis of marriage among the West-Mongolian Ööld after socialism, based on fieldworkd. As a major passage rite marriage continues to be an important principle structuring social relations even in post-socialist times. First, the scarce existing material on this topic is presented and the problem explained. Then, elementary classifications of nomadic cattle breeding societies (space, work, events/festivals) are described as context for the marriage ritual; this entails primarily ideas of *ordered space*, of hierarchical order according to age, status, and gender. The third chapter deals with the marriage process itself – and the chronological aspect of pre- and post-nuptial rites as well as the marriage ritual itself. At the end of each ‚ritual block' excursuses their specific topics are explained.

ZOTTER, ASTRID & CHRISTOF ZOTTER (Eds.)
Hindu and Buddhist initiations in India and Nepal
(Ethno-Indology. Heidelberg studies in South Asian rituals 10)
Wiesbaden: Harrassowitz Verlag 2010
380 pp., Euro 64,-; ISBN 3-447-06387-6

Keywords: initiation, Hindu initiations, Buddhist initiations, Bāhun, Chetri, upanayana, marriage, Newars, Urāy rituals, Tantrism, Śaiva Siddhānta, Vaiṣṇavas

##The volume at hand brings together the papers of the International Symposium "Hindu and Buddhist Initiations in India and Nepal" held at Heidelberg in May 2008. Sponsored by the German Research Foundation (Deutsche Forschungsgemeinschaft, DFG) and by the symposia program of the University of Heidelberg, this event was organized under the aegis of the Collaborative Research Centre (Sonderforschungsbereich) on Ritual Dynamics. Its purpose was to discuss changes in and interrelationships among different initiation rituals in South Asia and their relation to other kinds of rituals.##

ZOTTER, CHRISTOF: Notes on the Evolution of an Initiation Ritual: The *Vratabandha* of the Bāhun and Chetri

KEßLER-PERSAUD, ANNE: Economy and Composition of Complex Rituals: *Upanayana* and *Samāvartana* as Part of Nuptial Ceremonies

EINOO, SHINGO: Notes on *Āñjana*

GÖGGE, KATHLEEN: Early Childhood Rituals among the Newars and Parbatiyās in the Kathmandu Valley

MICHAELS, AXEL: Newar Hybrid Ritual and its Language in Hindu Initiations

GUTSCHOW, NIELS: The *Ihi* Marriage among the Newars of Bhaktapur, Nepal: Spatial Connotations of an Initiation Ritual

GELLNER, DAVID N.: Initiation as a Site of Cultural Conflict among the Newars

LEWIS, TODD T.: Ritual (Re-)Constructions of Personal Identity: Newar Buddhist Life-Cycle Rites and Identity among the Urāy of Kathmandu

ROSPATT, ALEXANDER VON: Remarks on the Consecration Ceremony in Kuladatta's *Kriyāsaṃgrahapañjikā* and its Development in Newar Buddhism

ISAACSON, HARUNAGA: Observations on the Development of the Ritual of Initiation (*abhiṣeka*) in the Higher Buddhist Tantric Systems

GENGNAGEL, JÖRG: Conversion or Initiation? On the Removal of the Sectarian Marks (*liṅgoddhāra*) in Śaiva Siddhānta

HÜSKEN, UTE: Challenges to a Vaiṣṇava Initiation?

COLAS, GERARD: *Pratiṣṭhā*: Ritual, Reproduction, Accretion

ZOTTER, ASTRID: How to Initiate a Tree: The *Aśvatthopanayana* in Prescriptive Texts

AUSTRALIA/OCEANIA

ANTONI, ALEXANDER DE
„Call us Kau, not Citak" Constitutive factors for the ethnic consciousness of an Asmat subgroup
Anthropos 105.2010:411-422
Keywords: Kau, Citak

##The names commonly applied to the ethnic group of the Kau until now have been determined by non-emic denotations. Besides this fact, concepts constitutive for the ethnic consciousness of the Kau will be dealt with. They take a significant position in the development of strategies for coping with the social environment in which the group is embedded. These concepts are transmitted through principles analogically coded into mythical motifs. In mythical presentations these ideas are passed on and conserved in a society. This process will be exemplified by means of Kau myths.##

BEDNARIK, ROBERT G.
Pleistocene rock art in Australia
Anthropos 105.2010:3-12
Keywords: Pleistocene, rock art, palaeoart, petroglyphs

##The occurrence of Pleistocene rock art in Australia is reviewed against the background of historical developments in the age estimation of rock art. Despite errors in interpreting data and the continuing paucity of credibly dated examples, it is apparent that most rock art of the earliest phase has survived as petroglyphs, which is consistent with the rest of the world. The author estimates that a large proportion of Australian petroglyphs are of the Pleistocene, and he points out that this corpus relates exclusively to Mode 3 (Middle Palaeolithic) technological traditions. It therefore follows that, contrary to conventional notions, which see palaeoart traditions commencing with the Aurignacian, there is actually far more surviving "Middle Palaeolithic" rock art in the world than there is "Upper

Palaeolithic." The Pleistocene rock art of Australia is very similar to the Middle Palaeolithic or Middle Stone Age petroglyphs of other continents.##

BEER, BETTINA
Ethnologie, Verwandtschaft und Kognitionswissenschaften
Zeitschrift für Ethnologie 135.2010:199-218
Keywords: cognitive sciences, kinship and cognitivism, Wampar, marriage, kin terms, hybridization, agency, practice

##*Sociocultural anthropology, kinship and cognitive sciences*
In this paper I analyse changes in the kinship terminology of the Wampar of Papua New Guinea (PNG) and address some problematic questions in cognitive anthropology. In recent decades, Wampar modes of social reproduction have changed as transcultural marriages, and the intercultural kindreds these produce, have increased. One manifestation of this is revealed by longitudinal data on kin terms; these also show how the blending of vernaculars and Tok Pisin (PNG's lingua franca) respond to the hybridizing effects of social life in this part of contemporary PNG. The formal semantic analysis of kinship terms was an important early focus of cognitive anthropology; as complex, systematic and shared realms of meaning, such terminologies were seen as paradigmatically cultural. Later, textual and agency-centred models became more popular than the formal semantic approaches. My analysis of changes to Wampar terms in the face of transformed relations between cultures is relevant to those interested in the connections between cognitive models and cultural practice. A focus on actors' choices of kin terms and behaviours in complex, culturally and linguistically heterogeneous settings that are well described ethnographically can help overcome the polarization between an emphasis on formal structural models and actor-centred case studies.##

ERCKENBRECHT, CORINNA
Zur wissenschaftlichen Rezeption des Fremden. Die australischen Aborigines in den Augen der Anthropologie und Ethnologie des 19. und 20. Jahrhunderts
Anthropos 105.2010:13-27

Keywords: Aborigines, evolutionism, physical anthropology, polygamy, structural functionalism, affluent society, noble savage

The scientific reception of the Other. Australian Aborigines in the eyes of 19th and 20 century anthropology

##This historical analysis shows how differently the Australian Aborigines, the social structure of their society, their physical appearance, their hunter-gatherer economy and their cultural artefacts were perceived, interpretcd, and categorized by European naturalists, (physical) anthropologists, missionaries and museum curators during the 19th and 20th century. Various aspects of Aboriginal culture were emphasized in academic theories depending on the scientific paradigms prevalent at the time and on the personal background of the respective author. This contribution suggests a new understanding of polygamous hunter-gatherer societies in Aboriginal Australia based on new indigenous film material##

FUNKE, JOACHIM
Kooperation zwischen Ethnologen und Psychologen: Optionen, Probleme, Visionen
Zeitschrift für Ethnologie 135.2010:249-258
Keywords: theory of mind, cognitive sciences, ‚universal development', psychology and anthropology

##Cooperation between anthropologists and psychologists: Options, problems, visions

Cooperation between anthropology and psychology is necessary for a deeper understanding of cultural specifics based on universal human minds. This paper describes one such cooperation in more detail, concerning the "Theory of Mind" (ToM) in the Pacific region. This theory predicts an attribution of mental states such as desires or beliefs to oneself and to others in the development of humans at the age of about 4 years. The universality of this assumption is tested by studies with children from Micronesia, Polynesia, and Papua New Guinea. The ToM paradigms from studies that were run originally in a European or American context had to be adapted carefully to local contexts. The benefits and risks of such an interdisciplinary cooperation are discussed.##

HENNINGS, WERNER
Räume, Orte, Botschaften. Mythologie, Geschichte und Gesellschaft Samoas im Spiegel räumlicher Strukturen und einer Theorie narrativer Räume
Sociologus 60.2010:163-190
Keywords: mythology, spatiality, narrative space, modernity, spatial symbols, anti-colonialism

##*Places and their meanings. Interpreting the structure of Samoan towns*
At the end of September, 2009, a tsunami destroyed many villages on the south coast of the island of Upolu. Spatial structures, however, constitute an archive of the society reflecting its social experience and culture. Based on the theoretical findings of Eco, Chomsky and Giddens, the paper first presents some elementary aspects of a theory of narrative places which sees architecture and spatial arrangements embedded in the wider framework of communication and language theories. Subsequently, the paper observes the spatial structures of two Samoan villages, the messages which emanate from these places and the meaning which these messages may have for the understanding of Samoan society änd culture. In their "spatial narration" both villages can be seen as "narrative spaces", their spatial texts appear as a mirror of Samoan mythology, history and social structure: Lepea tells of the history of the anti-colonial resistance movement, spatial symbol of the national identity, whereas the village of Poutasi tells the story of the social hierarchy of the village and of the Samoan turn to modernity, spatial symbol of a local identity.##

SCHINDLBECK, MARKUS
Der Federmantel von Hawai'i in der Berliner Sammlung
Baessler-Archiv 58.2010:139-158
Keywords: feather cloak, museology, gift exchange, art, cultural change, museology

The feather cloak of Hawai'i in the Berlin Collection
##The history of one of the most prominent pieces of the Oceanic collection in the Ethnologisches Museum Berlin, the feather cloak from Hawai'i, shows the different uses and interpretations which at ethnographic objects undergo through their long history in European museums. This appropriation of objects from a far distance, lateley as the feather assemblage for a modern art installation reducing the cloak to its material substance, has to be seen in a long and tormenting history of misunder-

standings and misallocations in the discourse between Hawaii and Europe. The feather cloak is also part of the culture change which occurred on these islands at the beginning of the 19th century and documents a history of these islands.##

STADLBAUER, JOHANNA
Projekt Selbstverwirklichung? Lebensentwürfe von Österreicherinnen in Neuseeland
Berlin: Mana Verlag 2010
175 pp., Euro 24.80; ISBN 3-93403166-8
Keywords: emigration, identity construction, voluntary migration, migration as self-realization

The project of self-realization? Blueprints of the life of female Austrians in New Zealand
Stadlbauer focuses on voluntary, i.e. life-style migration (as opposed to ,forced' migration as in cases of political harrassment, eviction, etc.), and she has interviewed 15 such migrants during a field trip. Basic motivation of these migrants was to lead a ,meaningful' life, which is subject to constant *bricolage* among the migrants. In Interviewing the people the author applies Roland Girtler's ,ero-epic' (free) conversation. Topics are politics of immigration and national identity of New Zealand, the history of emigration in Austria, movitations of the migrants, forms of ,self-realization' in New Zealand, and kinds of praxis of classification and delimitation used in the process of identity construction.

STASCH, RUPERT
The category ,village' in Melanesian social worlds. Some theoretical and methodological possibilities
Paideuma 56.2010:41-62
Keywords: villages

The main goal I pursue ... is to denaturalise the category ,village' itself, by giving an ethnographic account of life without villages, and of a contingent and ambivalent transition to life with them. But in the course of working on this topic, when I have sought comparative insights from colleagues and published literature (including work from Melanesia, India,

and Amazonia), I have often learned that other scholars have also been thoughtfully analysing villages as relational entities, including ‚even' in settings where villages are a longstanding cultural presence rather than a new and foreign one.##

EUROPE

BEYER, HEIKO & ULF LIEBE
Antiamerikanismus und Antisemitismus: Zum Verhältnis zweier Ressentiments
Zeitschrift für Soziologie 39.2010:215-232
Keywords: Anti-Americanism, Anti-Semitism, projection thesis, cognitive psychology, communication latency thesis

##Anti-Americanism and Anti-Semitism: On the relationship between two resentments
The present paper investigates the relationship between anti-American and anti-Semitic resentments on a terminological, theoretical, and empirical level. We start by identifying a set of shared structural principles drawn from historical research: personification of modernity, Manichaeism, and the construction of identitary collectives. On this basis established theories of anti-Semitism are applied to anti-Americanism. Following the projection thesis of critical theory and basic assumptions of cognitive psychology, anti-Americanism (together with other resentments) can be seen as a psychofunctional substitute for anti-Semitic attitudes in the process of channeling social discontent ("projection shift"). The communication latency thesis, on the other hand, suggests that anti-Americanism can appear as a vehicle for the communication of anti-Semitic attitudes ("detour communication"). Empirical support for both theoretical relationships is provided by an exemplary study of cross-section data from interviews with 241 pupils from Chemnitz, Dresden, and Leipzig (Germany).##

BLANKENBURG, WOLFGANG
Ethnopsychiatrie im Inland. Norm-Probleme im Hinblick auf die Kultur- und subkultur-Bezogenheit psychiatrischer Patienten
Curare 33,1/2.2010:42-52
Keywords: Ethno-psychiatry, Devereux, G., forensic psychiatry, psychosis, mental health problems, paranoia

##Ethno-psychiatry at home. Norm Problems of Psychiatric in-patients in Relation to Different Cultural Backgrounds
From a psychiatric view point the author demonstrates some case studies and shows the methodological problems how to distinguish psychopathological developments in migrants from false interpretations of culturally seeming differences. In the same time he warns to make cultural judgements by prejudices and pleas for an ethno-psychiatry at home.*##*

BOATCĂ, MANUELA
Grenzsetzende Macht. Geopolitische Strategien europäischer Identitätsbildung
Berliner Journal für Soziologie 20.2010:23-44

Keywords: boundaries, borders and power, power and borders, identity building, cultural difference, occidentalism, global power, asymmetric boundaries, nation states, space and essentialism

##Border-setting power - Geopolitical strategies of European identity building
Using a historical and comparative perspective, the present article argues that the politically most effective and strategically most enduring boundaries of modernity were not those between nation-states, but rather those whose orienting and identity building function were based on the maintenance of a power imbalance essentializing cultural, religious or economic differences. The main argument is that the historically unique power of definition, which has conferred validity to the different versions of the West/Rest or North/South explanatory models up to this day, can be traced back to two elements: on the one hand, to the constitutive relationship between Western notions of cultural difference and the global Western power ("Occidentalism"), on the other hand, to the universalizing perspective which in this power context was declared as the only valid scientific representation of space ("hubris of the zero point"). The historical and current impact of this discursive strategy for constructing essentialized spaces are shown using the examples of Latin America and Eastern Europe as typical products of asymmetric boundaries.*##*

BUKOW, WOLF-DIETRICH
Urbanes Zusammenleben. Zum Umgang mit Migration und Mobilität in europäischen Stadtgesellschaften
(Interkulturelle Studien 20)
Wiesbaden: VS Verlag 2010
261 pp., Euro 29.90; ISBN 3-531-17054-1

Keywords: urban coexistence, coexistence, postmodernity, integration, assimilation, diversity, division of labor, accomodation, everyday life

Urban coexistence. Dealing with migration and mobility in European urban societies
The author sees a competence of European urban societies to deal with diversity – an ability acquired through centuries. However, the debate on increasing diversity in the course of globalization is framed in a national discourse and national ideas (‚national narratives'). Starting point of the study is that successful urban coexistence is not a question of integration or assimilation but of an adequate application of mobility and division of labor. Bukow sees a necessity to focus on the ‚diversity competence' of urban societies in order to design society anew along these lines. Th second chapter discusses the importance of mobility in the beginning postmodern era, including the process from ‚informal to structural accomodation' of alterity, exemplified by using empirical material from Cologne. The author concludes that successful urban coexistence would be a question of well-understood (‚informed', experienced) routine – as has been proven in the historical case of European urban coexistence.

CZARNECKA, MIROSLAWA, THOMAS BORGSTEDT & TOMASZ JABLECKI (Eds.)
Frühneuzeitliche Stereotype. Zur Produktivität und Restriktivität sozialer Vorstellungsmuster. Jahrestagung der Internationalen Andreas Gryphius Gesellschaft Wroclaw 8. bis 11. Oktober 2008
(Jahrbuch für internationale Germanistik Reihe A. Kongressberichte 99)
Bern: Lang Verlag 2010
490 pp., Euro 94.10; ISBN 3-0343-0329-3

Keywords: national stereotypes, stereotypes, literature and stereotypes, gender stereotypes, Early modern stereotypes

Early modern stereotypes. On the productivity and restrictivity of social patterns of imagination. Annual meeting of the International Andreas Gryphius Society Wroclaw, October 8-11, 2008
The 24 papers in this volume are devoted to (European) national stereotypes, social stereotypes and literary texts. This includes topics like stereotypes regarding witches/witchcraft, images of the body, an stereotypes in specific literary works. So the papers also discuss the process of knowledge derived from experience, related to values, in various cultures, as well as gender stereotypes etc. The authors want to show how the stereotypes have been mediated in media of Early Modernity – in the arts, in literature, in emblematics etc.

DITTRICH, ECKHARD & INGRID OSWALD (Eds.)
Jenseits der Städte. Postsozialistische Lebensweisen in ländlichen Regionen Mittel- und Osteuropas
(Gesellschaftliche Transformationen/Societal transformations 16)
Berlin: Lit Verlag 2010
316 pp., Euro 24.90; ISBN 3-643-10308-6
Keywords: urbanism, ruralism, administration, post-socialist societies, failed states, self-administration

Beyond cities. Postsocialist lifestyles in rural areas of Central and Eastern Europe
The contributions in this volume have been funded by a research grant of the German Research Council (Deutsche Forschungsgemeinschaft).
DITTRICH, ECKHARD & INGRID OSWALD: Dörfliche Entwicklung und Strukturwandel in Ost(mittel)europa [Rural development and structural change in East-Central Europe]
OSWALD, INGRID & ECKHARD DITTRICH: Schichtende. Von der Schließung „industrialisierter Dörfer" in post-sozialistischen Gesellschaften [On the closing down of „industrialized villages" in post-socialist societies]
TOOMERE, TUULI: Gemeindeaktivierung in einem estnischen Dorf [Activating community life in an Estonian village]
NIKIFOROVA, ELENA: Der Verkauf der Schönheit. Anmerkungen zum „Re-Branding" von Dörfern in Estland [The selling of beauty. On the Re-branding of villages in Estonia]
JELEVA, RUMIANA & ECKHARD DITTRICH: Das bulgarische Dorf Z. [The Bulgarian village of Z.]

CHIKADZE, ELENA: Das zweite Leben eines alten Dorfes. Wie wir zur Auswahl unseres russischen Dorfes kamen [Second life of an old village. How we chose our Russian village]
BREDNIKOVA, OLGA: Das Dorf ist tot! - Es lebe das Dorf! Nochmals über den Unterschied zwischen Stadt und Land [On the difference between town and rural area]
BOGDANOVA, ELENA: Zur Anthropologie der „Zweistöcker" im Dorf. Anmerkungen zu einem misslungenen Staatsprojekt [On the anthropology of the „Two-stories" in the village. On a failed state project]
TIMOFEEVA, TATJANA: „Vom Wasser haben wir's gelernt" [„We learned it from the water"]
KASJANOVA, ALEKSANDRA & ALEKSANDR MANUJLOV: Wir handeln [We act]
ERNST, FRANK: Fernab der Städte: Leben auf dem Lande in Ostdeutschland [Far away from cities: Living in the countryside of Eastern Germany]
MARKARIAN, TATEVIK: Lokale Selbstverwaltung im post-sozialistischen Armenien. Informelle Beziehungen und öffentliche verwaltung in ländlichen Gemeinden [Local self-administration in post-socialist Armenia. Informal relations and public administration in rural communities]

GEHL, KATERINA
Übersetzung des „Fremden". Zur Vermittlung deutscher Dramen in Bulgarien 1870-1920
(Kulturgeschichtliche Perspektiven 8)
Berlin: Lit Verlag 2010
296 pp., Euro 29.90; ISBN 3-643-10418-2
Keywords: alterity, drama and alterity, standardization (EU), normalization (EU), national traditions, translations and culture

Translating the „Other". On the mediation of German drama in Bulgaria 1870-1920
This anthropological study in the area of Southeastern Europe focuses on the process of ‚Europeization' in Bulgaria after the Ottoman Empire using translations (of 1870-1920) of drama (old an new ones) of five decades. The focus is the analysis of everyday phenomena, and the author wants to show the (non-)appropriation of the „alien Europe" in the difference between the original texts and translations, such as the process of

„Bulgarization" of the young Bulgarian nation. This is of particular interest if one considers present processes of normalization and standardization in the European Union. So the comparison of original and translation is a study in cultural relations, or possible cultural relations, given that drama and theater are models of the reality of the respective cultures. Results show that the most remarkable deviations of translations from the original concern religious content, certain family and gender relations, differentiation of social strata, and positively vs. negatively depicted state institutions.

GRUNOW, HENDRIKJE
Es gibt keine Zufälle. Elvis lebt. Und die Apokalypse ist nah
Cargo. Zeitschrift für Ethnologie 30.2010:48-52
Keywords: homeless people, coincidence, homeless women

There is no coincidence. Elvis lives. And the apocalypse is near
This is a short field report on homeless women in Berlin, exemplified in one case which is biographically narrated.

HEMME, DOROTHEE
Harnessing Daydreams. A Library of Fragrant Fantasies
Ethnologia Europaea 40.2010:5-18
Keywords: perfume, daydreams, memory, rationalised scents, smelling, revelling, scents

##Smell works in many contexts as a trigger for fantasies: a scent reaches your nose surprisingly or familiarly and evokes memories and daydreams. Although associations with scents are extremely personal, they are also subject to conditioning factors that may be cultural, temporal or contextual. This paper traces conditioning factors and fantasies connected with smells by analysing the creations and marketing strategies of the Library of Fragrance, a company that commodifies the close relationship of smelling and daydreaming. What associations and atmospheres are chosen to be turned into perfume and how do perfumers find them? Which culturally constructed smell associations are profitable? How do individuals resist commodified scent-associations and where are the limits of instrumentalisation? Furthermore, what can we glean from smell regarding the practice of daydreaming?##

HINZ, THOMAS
Die Diffusion einer sozialen Bewegung - lokale Austauschnetzwerke in Deutschland
Zeitschrift für Soziologie 39.2010:60-80
Keywords: diffusion and exchange, exchange networks, networks, local exchange networks, trading systems, monetized economy, media and exchange

##*The Diffusion of a social Movement - Local Exchange Networks in Germany*
In the late 1980s and early 1990s a new social movement - the local exchange trading systems (LETS) - reached Germany. This initially Canadian movement draws attention to societal and economic failures of the monetized economy and attempts to resolve them on a local level. By introducing alternative local currency systems the exchange networks movement tries to promote a sustainable and local economy and aims at improving the living conditions of underprivileged people. Whereas founding activities were initially slow to emerge, a boom occurred in the mid 1990s. Our research describes the patterns of diffusion in German counties (Landkreise and kreisfreie Städte). In order to explain the diffusion process, we employ concepts of spatial proximity, the impact of national print media, and general socio-cultural fit. Finally, we analyze the effects of differently defined population densities on founding rates. Using data for the period from 1988 to 2005, we are able to confirm that social contagion and national print media are of considerable importance for the growth of these exchange systems. Furthermore, the roles of socio-cultural factors and of ecological assumptions are supported as well. In East Germany, diffusion takes place very slowly. We discuss this result with respect to the comparative lack of ideological resources.##

KAUTT, YORK
Televisuelle Koch-formate: Zur Kulturbedeutsamkeit eines Bereichs der Massenmedien
Sociologia Internationalis 48.2010:273-309
Keywords: cooking, TV cooking, mass media and cooking, entertainment and cooking

TV cookery formats: On the cultural significance of an area of mass media
##The objective of this article is to analyse whether the ongoing success of television cooking shows can be attributed to contemporary cultural systems and aspects of society. The analytical focus centres on the hypothesis that ways to communicate these TV formats contribute significantly to their own success story. Therefore, an empirical analysis is applied to explore the various incentives increasing the likelihood of recipient acceptance. A categorisation of ‚incentive structures' is employed to characterise cooking shows as a specific segment of mass media entertainment, and further to reveal the value and meaning of cooking and eating in the context of various cultural and societal dimensions of the focused formats. Thus, based on the research findings produced in this paper, the article aims to analyse the specific roles of cooking shows in our contemporary societies.##

KOVÁCS, ADORJÁN F.
Patronage und Geld. Schließungsmechanismen bei der Besetzung von Lehrstühlen am Beispiel einer wissenschaftlichen Teildisziplin in Deutschland
Berliner Journal für Soziologie 20.2010:499-526
Keywords: patronage, scientific patronage, clientelism, academic caste system, appointment procedures, closure, inclusion, exclusion

##*Patronage and money. Closure mechanisms in the appointment of chairs using the example of a scientific subdiscipline in Germany*
In the light of the increasing political influence on German universities (amongst others, the excellence initiative) with effects on the selection of top positions, this article examines the appointment of chairs (department heads) in a "small" surgical specialty during the last 30 years. Following the delineation of official indicators of competence (inclusion criteria) within an appointment procedure, it can be shown that a broad distribution of institutions and persons that meet these criteria exists. The empirical examination of the actually successful occupations shows that closure mechanisms play a role because the successful candidates stem from no more than 10 out of 34 clinical departments. The monetary capital in terms of third-party funds is the most important allocation criterion, but cannot sufficiently explain the way appointments take place. As there are candidates who in formal terms are in a wide measure equally qualifled, and a consequential uncertainty of the basis of decision within an

appointment procedure, the derivation of the candidate in terms of a personal relationship to a chair holder (department head) from whose clinic he applies and who acts as a patron, proves to be the decisive distinction following the examination of all inclusion criteria. This results in a reproduction of the chair holders (department heads) largely from the same clinical departments and the formation of an academic caste system. In perspective, this cartel-like closure appears to be getting increasingly worse.##

LANGENOHL, ANDREAS
Imaginäre Grenzen. Zur Entstehung impliziter Kollektivität in EU-Europa
Berliner Journal für Soziologie 20.2010:45-63
Keywords: borders, imaginary borders, collectivities

##*Imaginary borders: The emergence of implicit collectivities in EU-Europe*
Drawing on a practice-theoretical approach inspired by the notion of the social imaginary, imaginary borders in the European Union are conceptualized as the public emergence, maintenance and modification of interpretations about European borders through practices of circulation of symbols, commodities, and people. The construction of borders in the EU is thus neither located on the attitudinal level nor conceived of as the deliberate construction of meaning, but as the unintended emergence of the border as a meaningful category from taken-for-granted practices carrying their own meaning. Focusing on twin towns' activities in the European Union as a paradigmatic location for the articulation of political-cultural understandings of the EU, it is argued that these articulations are not only embedded within economic and social circuits, but in the first place emerge from them as taken-for-granted and imaginary meanings of what the EU as a polity is and where its borders are. Methodologically, this calls for an understanding of the relationship between imaginary political collectivity and its economic, social and cultural channels of circulation which is not conceived as a text-context-relation but as one of mutual imaginary constitution.##

LORENZ, ROBERT
„ Wir bleiben in Klitten" Zur Gegenwart in einem ostdeutschen Dorf
(Europäische Ethnologie 8)
Berlin: Lit Verlag 2008
163 pp., Euro 19.90; ISBN 3-8258-1644-5
Keywords: rural life, agency in villages, change and agency, action theory, local agency

„ We will stay in Klitten" On contemporary life in an East German village
This village was was destined to be removed for brown coal mining in this
area in the days of the GDR but managed to survive during the political
upheavals and changes of 1989, when the Iron Curtain fell. The village
managed to do well through the 1990, but then problems began to show
when the population declined. This study follows these processes of village
community from an actors' point of view asking for local agency in the
rural periphery of Eastern Germany. The text is very much based on
interview texts which make up about half of the book.

PICKEL, GERT
*Säkularisierung, Individualisierung oder Marktmodell? Religiosität und
ihre Erklärungsfaktoren im europäischen Vergleich*
Kölner Zeitschrift für Soziologie und Sozialpsychologie 62.2010:219-245
Keywords: secularization, individualization, market model, religious vitality

*##Secularization, individualization or market model? - Religious vitality
and their sources in European comparison*
The debates of the religious development in the last decades have
uncovered the differences of the current theories of the sociology of
religion. Most of them point out different explanations of the developments
of religiosity and involvement in church in the unified Europe, often
combined with a critique of the traditional dominant secularization theory.
In the article on the hand, a quantitative analysis of the religious vitality in
Europe, focused mainly on the macro-level, using a combination of a wide
range of survey data, will be conducted. The results lead to the assumption,
that the secularization theory should not be rejected too fast. But its general
assumptions have to be framed in cultural context, to be useful for a
continuing explanation of religious vitality in Europe. The cultural-
historical influence of dominant religions, the political framework or
results of political repression and processes of identity formation play
important roles. Including these factors, it seems to be possible, to explain

the differences in religious vitality in Europe. Especially, the conflicting effects of the framework of Eastern European religion are of special interest.##

PUTTKAMER, JOACHIM JESKO VON & GABRIELLA SCHUBERT (Eds.)
Kulturelle Orientierungen und gesellschaftliche Ordnungsstrukturen in Südosteuropa
(Forschungen zu Südosteuropa. Sprache – Kultur – Literatur 4)
Wiesbaden: Harrassowitz Verlag 2010
253 pp., Euro 54,-; ISBN 3-447-06243-5

Keywords: assembly (right of), order, structures of order, collectivity, individualism, heroism, literature and politics, conflict, metawars, modernization, democracy, corruption

Cultural orientation and societal structures of order in Southeastern Europe
The papers of this volume are based on a conference in 2008 and discuss problems of the ‚Europeization' of the Balkans in the post-socialist era.
PUTTKAMER, JOACHIM VON & GABRIELLA SCHUBERT: Kulturelle Orientierungen und gesellschaftliche Ordnungsstrukturen in Südosteuropa. Zur Einführung [Introduction]
GIORDANO, CHRISTIAN: Südosteuropa - eine Region eigener Art? [Southeastern Europe – A region of its own kind?]
RAECKE, JOCHEN: Kollektivität und Individualität als literarische Leitbilder – oder Wenn kollektives Heldentum (der Männer) nur individuelles Leid (der Frauen) bedeutet (wie im Kosovozyklus) [Collectivity and individuality as literary guidelines]
SCHUBERT, GABRIELLA: Literarische Entwürfe interethnischen Zusammenlebens [Literary outlines of interethnic communal life]
PANI, PANDELI: „Die Spannung dieser Zeit ist nicht in Ordnung... Oder muss man den ganzen Generator tauschen?" Literarische Verarbeitung des Systemumbruchs in der albanischen und bulgarischen Literatur [Literary assimilation of systemic change in Albanian and Bulgarian literature]
MAKRIDES, VASILIOS N.: Gemeinschaftlichkeitsvorstellungen in Ost- und Südosteuropa und die Rolle der orthodox-christlichen Tradition [Ideas of conviviality in Eastern and Southeastern Europe and the role of the Orthodox-Christian tradition]

ROTH, KLAUS: Alltagsmuster der Arbeitswelt in der Transformation [Everyday patterns of the world of labor during the transformation] AXT, HEINZ-JÜRGEN: Konflikte in Südosteuropa [Conflict in Southeastern Europe] SUNDHAUSEN, HOLM: Metakriege. Kriegserfahrung und Kriegsbewältigung im ehemaligen Jugoslawien [Metawars. Experience and coping of/with war in former Yugoslavia] STERBLING, ANTON: Unterschiedliche Modernisierungsverläufe in Ungarn und Rumänien nach 1989? [Differing pathways of modernization in Hungary and Romania after 1989?] SZABO, MATE: Defizite der Demokratie oder Machtausübung mit Defiziten? Probleme der Kundgebungen und des Versammlungsrechts in Ungarn [Deficits of democracy, or practice of power with deficits? Problems of proclamations and of the right of assembly in Hungary] GABANYI: ANNELI UTE: Korruptionsbekämpfung in Rumänien und Bulgarien [Fighting corruption in Romania and Bulgaria]

REICHERTZ, JO et al. (Eds.)
Jackpot. Erkundungen zur Kultur der Spielhallen. 2. Auflage
(Erlebniswelten 16)
Wiesbaden: VS Verlag 2010
237 pp., Euro 14.90; ISBN 3-531-17606-2
Keywords: jackpot, gambling, sociology of gambling, participant observation, compulsive gambling

Jackpot. Exploring the culture of gambling arcades. 2nd ed.
In this sociological study the culture of gambling in German gambling arcades is described and analyzed, using participant observation and ‚observing participation‘, conversations, analyses of documents. Thus, the authors reconstruct the social order the gamblers are confronted with, how they appropriate it, and how, in this way, they re-create gambling hall culture anew. It has become explicit that culture in gambling arcades can be characterized with notions such as ‚challenge‘ and ‚proving oneself‘ much better thant with ‚gambling for money‘ and ‚compulsive gambling‘.

ROSSBACH DE OLMOS, LIOBA
Santería in Deutschland. Zur Gleichzeitigkeit von Heterogenisierung und Retraditionalisierung einer Religion in der Diaspora
Paideuma 56.2010:63-86
Keywords: Santería, diaspora, heterogenization, retraditionalization

Santería in Germany. On the simulaneity of heterogenization and retraditionalization of a religion in the diaspora
The article summarizes the contradictory panorama of heterogenization and simultaneous retraditionalization, based on several years of fieldwork, applying ,multi-sited ethnography' almost, since individual practitioners living dispersed had to be found.

RÜSSMANN, KIRSTEN, SIMON M. DIERKES & PAUL B. HILL
Soziale Desintegration und Bindungsstil als Determinanten von Fremden-feindlichkeit
Zeitschrift für Soziologie 39.2010:281-301
Keywords: disintegration, attachment style, xenophobia, avoidance, anxiety

##*Social Disintegration and Attachment Style as Determinants of Xenophobia*
This paper investigates whether xenophobic attitudes in Germany are determined by personal characteristics and by individual social situations. To this end, the influence on xenophobia of attachment style as a personal characteristic and of social disintegration as a variable of the social structure is tested. The analysis of a sample of 1779 persons indicates that aftachment styles can be considered as predispositions for the occurrence or not of social disintegration, which simultaneously determines the extent of xenophobia (complete mediation): a secure attachment style decreases the degree of social disintegration which then reduces the extent of xenophobic attitudes. An insecure attachment style induces an increasing degree of social disintegration and xenophobia. A consideration of the subscales "anxiety" and "avoidance" and of categorical values of attachment style (secure, anxious-preoccupied, fearful-avoidant, dismissive-avoidant) specifies this finding. The extent of avoidance and the fearful-avoidant attachment style are particularly important for the effects which we were able to identify.##

SCHMIDT, IRIS
„Zur raschen Erledigung etwaiger Beschwerden behülflich" Die Fürsorgetätigkeit des Hamburger Nachweisungsbüros für das Auswanderungswesen (1855-1914)
(TRANS. anthropologische texte 11)
Berlin: Lit Verlag 2010
99 pp., Euro 19.90; ISBN 3-643-10679-7
Keywords: emigration, middlemen and emigration, supervision of emigration

„At your service for rapidly solving possible complaints." The service function of the Hamburg office for tracing emigrations (1855-1914)
This government office at the service of emigrants had functions of controlling, helping and advising in the process of emigration. Before this, emigrants were often victims of fraudulent practices of business men mediating in the process of emigration. Using archival material the author asks whether the practice of this office adequately served the emigrants and how the office's control function affected the business of emigration. For this purpose, there is a descriptive historical account on emigration in Hamburg in the 19th and early 20th centuries, description of laws on emigration, private service organizations, and an account of the above-mentioned office itself.

SCHNEICKERT, CHRISTIAN & ALEXANDER LENGER
Studentische Hilfskräfte im deutschen Bildungswesen
Berliner Journal für Soziologie 20.2010:203-224
Keywords: student assistents, labor conditions, precarious employment, employment in universities

The situation of graduate assistants in the German higher educational system
The article takes a critical look at the situation of graduate assistants at German universities. For this purpose the paper is based on two sociological perspectives. On the one hand, being employed as a student assistant can be regarded as an important individual strategy to gather privileges in the German higher educational system. On the other hand, working as a student assistant is a paradigmatic example of labor conditions in modern society due to the fact that higher qualified persons need to be profoundly flexible and have to work under precarious employment conditions. The analysis highlights that the problematic

working conditions of student assistants are caused by the specific structures of the German education system. It is the difference between individual prospects and objective possibilities which makes these precarious labor conditions possible.##

SCHULZ, FLORIAN, JAN SKOPEK & HANS-PETER BLOSSFELD
Partnerwahl als konsensuelle Entscheidung. Das Antwortverhalten bei Erstkontakten im Online-Dating
Kölner Zeitschrift für Soziologie und Sozialpsychologie 62.2010:485-515
Keywords: mate selection, online dating, homophily, marriage market, dating behavior, consensus and mate selection, trade-off hypothesis

##Mate selection as a mutual choice – How men and women reply to contact offers im online dating
This study continues our analyses of contacting behavior in online dating (KZfSS 2/2009). As the beginning and continuation of a relationship is based on consensual decisions of both partners to interact, we concentrate on the question if and how potential partners indeed reply to contact offers. Data from online dating platforms therefore offer a unique opportunity for sociologists to study how partnerships are initiated and how they develop over time. This contribution provides four important empirical results: Firstly, it demonstrates that only 20% of all first contact offers are answered. This is a surprisingly small proportion. Secondly, it supports the hypothesis of homophily. According to this hypothesis, people with similar education, age and physical attractiveness should prefer each other and thus are more likely to form couples. Third, it shows that women still have severe problems to reply to contact offers from lower educated men, while men are already less reluctant to reply to higher educated women. Thus, the rarity of couples where women are higher educated than their partners are to a large proportion the consequence of women's preferences rather than men's preferences. Finally, our study does not find any support for the trade-off hypothesis, indicating that women do not exchange their physical attractiveness for men's educational resources, and vice versa.##

SPIELMANN, YVONNE
Hybridkultur
(Suhrkamp Taschenbuch Wissenschaft 1972)
Frankfurt/M.: Suhrkamp Verlag 2010
293 pp., Euro 12,-; ISBN 3-518-29572-4

Keywords: hybridation, media and hybridation, Manga comics, aesthetics, interculturality, transculturality, culture criticism, globalization

Hybrid culture
The motto of this book is that in the hybrid the connecting power dominates the separating power in unequal, or asymmetrical constellations. Spielmann discusses hybrid culture in specific ,ethnographic' aesthetic-tehcnical cases in Japan, based on ,field research' in 2005/06, but also in a general, abstract way suited for theory building. The examples deal with computer-based products that may be classified with western notions of ,artistic', or graphic/design products which in emic understanding have a predominantly intention of technical precision (p.8). Spielmann thus deals with present phenomena of numerous influences and components in this field of media, cultural contexts, and discoursive backgrounds. These are currently ,discussed' in cyberspace and multiple identity concepts. Spielmann proposes a critical notion of hybridation which makes media discourses and debates in Cultural Studies interdisciplinarily productive. Central is the thesis that hybridation is an up-to-date strategy of aesthetic intervention into internationally active media industries.

SPOHN, WILLFRIED
Europäische multiple Modernität als interzivilisatorische Konstellation. Zur Transformation Europas durch europäische Integration und Erweiterung in einer sich globalisierenden Welt
Berliner Journal für Soziologie 20.2010:5-22

Keywords: modernity, multiple modernities, European modernity, inter-civilizational relations

##European multiple modernity as an intercivilisational constellation – The transformation of Europe through European integration and enlargement in a globalizing world
In interdisciplinary and sociological research on Europe, Euro-centric modernization premises are still dominant, i.e, the explanation of the European multi-level regime on the basis of transnational spill-over

mechanisms originating from modernizing national societies in Europe. In contrast this article will outline an inter-civilizational multiple modernities approach to Europe, based on the work of Shmuel Eisenstadt. Such an approach needs to focus on: 1. the multiplicity of modernization trajectories and modernities, particuiarly in view of the transformation processes in postcommunist Central and Eastern Europe; 2. the international and inter-civilizational relations and encounters between European and non-European civilizational complexes; and 3. the global role of Europe and the global impact on Europe in a globalizing world. Only in considering such an inter-civilizational and global context is it possible to adequately conceptualize, analyze and explain the dynamics of the European integration and enlargement process.##

STÜLB, MAGDALENA
Transkulturelle Akteurinnen. Eine medizinethnologische Studie zu Schwangerschaft, Geburt und Mutterschaft von Migrantinnen in Deutschland
(Berliner Beiträge zur Ethnologie 20)
Berlin: Weißensee Verlag 2010
292 pp., Euro 24,-; ISBN 3-89998-176-6
Keywords: migrants and childbirth, childbirth of migrants, culture and childbirth

Transcultural actors. A medical-anthropological study on pregnancy, childbirth, and maternity of migrants in Germany
The author deals with the challenges and possible cultural conflict around the complex of obstetrics. She worked with women of various cultures during pregnancy, childbirth, and the first postnatal months. One basic observation was that these women related to knowledge, experiences and traditions of their respective countries, but they simultaneously used many other sources of information and systems of help to them. Neighbors, friends and family members have been transcultural networks helping them. The author also found that midwives have access and use manifold systems of knowledge and have their individual concepts of ‚good birth'. Thus, there is a transcultural space where both ‚parties' meet, exchange views, and create new aspects.

TAUSCHEK, MARKUS
Wertschöpfung aus Tradition. Der Karneval von Binche und die Konstituierung kulturellen Erbes
(Studien zur Kulturanthropologie/Europäischen Ethnologie 3)
Berlin: Lit Verlag 2010
351 pp., Euro 29.90; ISBN 3-643-10266-9
Keywords: carnival, cultural heritage, performative culture, UNESCO, world heritage, knowledge production, value generation, immaterial culture, representing values, intangible heritage, folklore, heritage production

Creating net product out of tradition. The carnival of Binche and the constitution of cultural heritage
Since the UNESCO discovered ‚performative culture' the immaterial heritage is in the focus of societal, scholarly, and political interest. Tauschek traces the conflict-ridden processes which constitute ‚cultural heritage', using the attempt to establish the carnival of Binche, Belgium, as a case of ‚world heritage', describing historically preconditioned modi of value generation influencing the present discourse on the utilization of immaterial culture. In this context, the meaning of the culture of tradition in late modernity is discuassed. The author first discusses cultural heritage as a field of study, then the politics of cultural heritage – national and international discourses, cultural heritage as production of knowledge, the historical genesis of creating values, and the question whether there are new cultural practices in the case of creating carnival as ‚world heritage'.

THIMM, TATJANA
Indische Touristen in Deutschland
Asien 114/115.2010:114-121
Keywords: tourism in Germany, Indian tourists

Indian tourists in Germany
##Tourists from India to Germany are becoming more and more of interest for scientific research since their numbers are on the upswing. This article focuses on structures and trends regarding tourism from India to Germany/Europe and delivers a profile of the Indian tourists in Germany.##

PERIODICALS SCANNED

Abhandlungen und Berichte des Staatlichen Museums für Völkerkunde
    Dresden
Afrika Spectrum (Africa Spectrum 45,1-3.2010)
Anthropos (105.2010)
Archiv für Völkerkunde
Asien (114/115.2010; 116.2010; 117.2010)

Baessler Archiv (58.2010)
Berliner Blätter. Ethnographische und ethnologische Beiträge. Sonderheft
Berliner Journal für Soziologie (20.2010)

Cargo - Zeitschrift für Ethnologie (30.2010)
Curare (34,1/2.2010)
Curare Sonderband

Entwicklungsethnologie. Zeitschrift d. Arbeitsgemeinschaft Entwicklungs-
    ethnologie
Erwägen Wissen Ethik (21.2010)
Etnofoor
Ethnologia Balkanica. Journal for Southeast Eureopean Anthropology
Ethnologia Europaea (40.2010)

Indiana (27.2010)
Internationales Asienforum (41.2010)

Kölner Zeitschrift für Soziologie und Sozialpsychologie (62.2010)

Mitteilungen aus dem Museum für Völkerkunde Leipzig
Mitteilungen der Berliner Gesellschaft für Anthropologie, Ethnologie und
    Urgeschichte
Mitteilungen des Museums für Völkerkunde Hamburg
Münchner Beiträge zur Völkerkunde

Paideuma (56.2010)
POP. Kultur und Kritik

Sociologia Internationalis (48.2010)
Sociologus (60.2010)

Tribus (59.2010)
Tsantsa. Revue de la Societé Suisse d'ethnologie (15.2010)

Zeitschrift für Ethnologie (135.2010)
Zeitschrift für Kulturaustausch (60.2010)
Zeitschrift für Soziologie (39.2010)
Zeitschrift für Volkskunde

AUTHOR INDEX

SUBJECT INDEX

Anthropological Abstracts

Cultural/Social Anthropology from German-speaking countries
edited by Ulrich Oberdiek

Anthropological Abstracts

Cultural / Social Anthropology
from German-speaking countries

Vol. 7.2008

LIT

Anthropological Abstracts

Cultural / Social Anthropology
from German-speaking countries

Vol. 6.2007

LIT

Anthropological Abstracts 7/2008

Anthropological Abstracts (AA) is a reference
journal published once a year in print, but also under
www.anthropology-online.de and announces – in English
language – most publications in the field of cultural/social
anthropology published in the German language area
(Austria, Germany, Switzerland). Since many of these publications have been written in German, and most German
publications are not included in the major English language
abstracting services, Anthropological Abstracts offers a
convenient source of information for anthropologists and
social scientists in general who do not read German, to become aware of anthropological research and publications in
German-speaking countries. Included are journal articles,
monographs, anthologies, exhibition catalogs, yearbooks,
etc. Most abstracts are authored by the editor, others are
specified accordingly. This journal is edited by Ulrich
Oberdiek since 1993 (formerly: Abstracts in German Anthropology; since 2002: *Anthropological Abstracts*).
Bd. 7, 2011, 224 S., 39,90 €, br., ISBN 978-3-643-99896-5

Anthropological Abstracts 6/2007

Anthropological Abstracts (AA) is a reference
journal published once a year in print, but also under
www.anthropology-online.de and announces – in English
language – most publications in the field of cultural/social
anthropology published in the German language area
(Austria, Germany, Switzerland). Since many of these publications have been written in German, and most German
publications are not included in the major English language
abstracting services, Anthropological Abstracts offers a
convenient source of information for anthropologists and
social scientists in general who do not read German, to become aware of anthropological research and publications in
German-speaking countries. Included are journal articles,
monographs, anthologies, exhibition catalogs, yearbooks,
etc. Most abstracts are authored by the editor, others are
specified accordingly. This journal is edited by Ulrich
Oberdiek since 1993 (formerly: Abstracts in German Anthropology; since 2002: *Anthropological Abstracts*).
Bd. 6, 2010, 176 S., 39,90 €, br., ISBN 978-3-643-10905-7

LIT Verlag Berlin – Münster – Wien – Zürich – London

Auslieferung Deutschland / Österreich / Schweiz: siehe Impressumsseite